Studies in Rhetorics and Feminisms

Series Editors, Cheryl Glenn and Shirley Wilson Logan

APPROPRIATE[ING] DRESS

Appropriate[ing] Dress: Women's Rhetorical Style in Nineteenth-Century America

Carol Mattingly

Southern Illinois University Press
Carbondale and Edwardsville

Library of Congress Cataloging-in-Publication Data

Mattingly, Carol, 1945–
    Appropriate[ing] dress : women's rhetorical style in nineteenth
        century America / Carol Mattingly.
        p. cm. — (Studies in rhetorics and feminisms)
    Includes bibliographical references and index.
        1. Speeches, addresses, etc., American—Women authors—History
    and criticism. 2. Rhetoric—Social aspects—United States—
    History—19th century. 3. Clothing and dress—United States—
    History—19th century. 4. Feminism--United States—History—19th
    century. 5. Women orators—United States. I. Title: Appropriating
    dress. II. Title. III. Series.

PS407 .M38 2002
808.5'1'082097309034—dc21
ISBN 0-8093-2428-8 (alk. paper)   2001034169

The paper used in this publication meets the minimum requirements of American National
Standard for Information Sciences—Permanence of Paper for Printed Library Materials,
ANSI Z39.48-1992. ♾

For Amy

Contents

Figures

Preface

As nineteenth-century women began to challenge restrictions against their public presence, the primary features that reflected their gendered positioning came into bold relief. Women were identified as feminine primarily according to the visual presentation of their bodies, especially with regard to dress, and according to location, a specifically assigned sphere. These complementary perceptions served to make women's assumption of public platforms and roles especially difficult. With specific attention to rhetoric, *Appropriate[ing] Dress: Women's Rhetorical Style in Nineteenth-Century America* examines the balancing of these intersections of location and "feminine" style. It explores ways in which women speakers used appearance to negotiate expectations restricting them to limited locations and excluding them from public rhetoric in order to challenge and reconstruct the power hierarchy.

The introduction, "Fabricated Gender," provides a historical context of the relation between gender and dress and situates the study within recent scholarship in the history of women and rhetoric. Chapter 1, "Friendly Dress: A Disciplined Use," explores early-nineteenth-century women speakers' appropriation of religious associations inherent in Quaker dress for establishing moral character as a means for furthering their ethical effectiveness. The Quaker religion contributed to women's preparation for public presentation, both mentally and rhetorically; at the same time, many women recognized the rhetorical importance of a style of dress that evoked moral and religious images. This chapter examines early-nineteenth-century women speakers' use of dress in their attempts to achieve rhetorical effectiveness, from the problematic efforts of Frances Wright to the more successful strategies of Angelina and Sarah Grimké and Abby Kelley Foster.

By the 1850s, curiosity associated with radical clothing provided a means by which some women drew large crowds to hear their messages and to make audiences familiar with the image of women speakers. Such breaching of gender constraints associated with appearance echoes those onerous efforts enacted by Frances Wright early in the century; however, many women in the 1850s effectively exploited interest in radical dress in forging national and international reputations that served their effectiveness as speakers. Chapter 2, "Blooming Celebrity: The Flowering of a National Ethos," examines manners in which the reform dress served women's rhetorical purposes at midcentury.

In the pre-electronic nineteenth century, news traveled most quickly via the print media. Newspapers disseminated information about current events quickly with editorial comments on their propriety. Fashion periodicals, a primary constructor of women's bodily image in the nineteenth century, related supplementary detail with regard to women's "proper" place and role. Widely read, these periodicals became the authority on appropriate dress for "ladies." Many combined expensive color fashion plates with intricate descriptions of the ornamentation of the clothing they presented (almost always of Parisian design) and its appropriate time of day and location. Rhetors had to contend with this strong construction, but even more problematic, the periodicals struggled to maintain their ascendancy in establishing norms of dress. Chapter 3, "Restraining Women's Rhetoric: Backlash Against the Reform Dress," looks at the rhetoric periodicals employed as they labored to discredit women's efforts to appropriate the dress conversation.

Chapter 4, "The Language of Passing and Desire: The Rhetoric of Cross-Dressing," looks at some women's use of traditional masculine clothing throughout the second half of the nineteenth century. Beginning at midcentury, women increasingly appropriated men's dress for numerous reasons. They might assume masculine dress for purposes of attending functions forbidden to women, from scheduled events to simply frequenting saloons and participating in night life. Some did so to avoid the cost of female attire at such social functions as theater performances and operas. Performers and professional women, from actress Charlotte Cushman to physician and rhetor Mary E. Walker, often manifested their masculine attire in a more open manner. This chapter seeks to understand the motivation and effects of such appropriation.

During the 1870s and 1880s, women more often used dress to undermine criticism of their public stance by presenting a feminine, but not ostentatious, appearance. Chapter 5, "[Re]Fashioning a Proper Image by Dressing the Part," looks at women's rhetoric of dress during this period. The most impressive women rhetors effected a "womanly" stance to disarm critics who accused them of being "unsexed" and to assuage a public that feared a danger to family and society. These rhetors nonetheless clearly understood the performative value associated with their bodily presentation. Chapter 5 explores the purposeful attention to dress and appearance that mollified critics and gained positive press coverage for women speakers, examining the strategic balancing act they negotiated.

The conclusion, "Dress and Body as Spectacle," explores the dress issue through notions of spectatorship. The incredible attention given to women's dress in the nineteenth century and men's efforts to determine the fashioning of that dress create an interesting relationship with late-twentieth-century definitions of pleasure related to visions of women's bodies.

The spectatorial is only one way of acknowledging the impact of dress for the nineteenth-century woman. Scholars continue to acknowledge its importance for nineteenth-century women speakers in other ways, whether consciously or not. Another obvious example is the newly unveiled sculpture of Lucretia Mott, Susan B. Anthony, and Elizabeth Cady Stanton for the 150th anniversary of the 1848 Seneca Falls Convention. Sculptor A. E. "Ted" Aub demonstrates Anthony's and Stanton's independence in Anthony's holding her gloves rather than wearing them and in Stanton's rolled-up sleeves. As we continue to acknowledge and use dress for demonstrating ethos in the twenty-first century, an examination of such complements to traditional rhetorical studies will help us to more fully understand women rhetors of other centuries.

Acknowledgments

*I*n completing this book, I have enjoyed the support of generous colleagues at Louisiana State University. Angeletta Gourdine and Susannah Brietz Monta have read and advised me on numerous drafts. Robin Roberts also read portions of the text. Janine Conant provided a constant source of support, clerical assistance, and encouragement that allowed for humor even at frustrating times. I wish to acknowledge my appreciation as well to the staffs at the interlibrary borrowing office and microfilm reading room at LSU's Middleton Library and to Leslie Beard in the LSU English Department for much appreciated assistance. As I finished this project at the University of Louisville, colleagues Karen Chandler, Ben Hufbauer, and Susan Ryan offered readings that improved the manuscript immensely.

I am grateful as well to Marc Bousquet and Anthony Monta for insights on William Bentley Fowle and Charles Lamb, respectively. I appreciate advice I received in the final stages of manuscript preparation from Catherine Hobbs, reader for Southern Illinois University Press, Karl Kageff and Carol Burns at the press, and copyeditor Elaine Durham Otto. For permission to reprint a revised version of "Friendly Dress: A Disciplined Use" 29 (Spring 1999): 25–45, I gratefully acknowledge *Rhetoric Society Quarterly.* Finally, I wish to recognize and thank Cheryl Glenn for her detailed suggestions for revision.

For support in all my pursuits, academic and otherwise, my loving appreciation to my daughters, sisters, and nieces. You bring much joy to my life.

Appropriate[ing] Dress

Introduction: Fabricated Gender

[C]an anybody tell me why reporters, in making mention of lady speakers, always consider it to be necessary to report, fully and *firstly,* the dresses worn by them?

—Fanny Fern

*I*n the above epigraph, taken from her June 18, 1870, column for the *New York Ledger,* "Lady Lecturers," Fanny Fern highlights the inordinate amount of attention given to two primary and intersecting components that formed gender identification for women. First, gender, inscribed on and around women's bodies, was constructed largely in the visual impact created by their clothing and appearance. Second, gender aligned women with location, a specifically assigned "sphere." Fern's observations about the focus on public women's appearance characterizes practices prevalent throughout the nineteenth-century United States, as a strictly fabricated image became the primary focus for those responding to and reporting on women activists. The remark highlights the gendered nature of perceptions about women's power and place, a duality that until recently excluded women from the historical tradition in rhetoric.

The gendered component of rhetoric complicates the historical picture in numerous ways as reflected in scholarship during the late twentieth century. Following Karlyn Kohrs Campbell's important pioneer volumes on women speakers, feminists in the history of rhetoric have called for further work in redressing imbalances in the rhetorical canon. For example, Patricia Bizzell has suggested several ways the rhetorical tradition might include women: resisting readings of traditional rhetorical history, recovering women and inserting them into the canon, and looking in new places and for new ways to redefine rhetoric ("Feminist Methods"). Similarly, Cheryl Glenn has called for a remapping or regendering of that tradition which will involve "our rethinking texts, approaches, narrative—and history itself" (3). The past decade has seen a heartening number of scholars add to our knowledge and understanding of the many women rhetoricians who had been relegated to obscure or forgotten niches. But rewriting/regendering the tradition can be problematic. Some scholars have expressed concern that "the visions of what constitute male and female experience appeal to or incorporate existing normative definitions" (Scott 4); that recovery projects may "support the presumption that the *majority* of women cannot rival male accomplishments" (Biesecker 142); or that "it is only when women are behaving in ways usually regarded as masculine—that is, politically and collectively—that they merit historical discussion" (Gordon, Buhle, and Dye 77).

Many feminist scholars share these concerns, recognizing that gender has been a primary feature in the shaping of our own understanding and that we are products of a strongly gendered tradition which has recognized only masculine bodies as important landmarks. Even as scholars have discovered women's bodies on the rhetorical landscape, they have sometimes valued those bodies according to existing standards; that is, they have measured women rhetors' worth by their ability to negotiate the trails forged by men. Despite some fears of creating a Great Woman counterpoint to the Great Man tradition, however, most have come to treasure our new understandings of the rich and previously buried tradition in women's rhetoric. This newly found heritage gives women a fuller sense of self as they come to identify with and appreciate their rhetorical foremothers and their locations on that map.

Most feminist historians of rhetoric want to continue the search for women's traditions, all the while recognizing the need to question and see in new ways—"through the lens of feminist perspectives" (Foss, Griffin, and Foss 1). Thus, most recently, feminist historians, recognizing the "disagreement over how to reconceive rhetorical theory and history" (Wertheimer 3), have accepted that there is "no one prescription for feminist revision" (Miller 373). Further, because controversy within our discipline is "mostly an artifact, being instigated by a genre of scholarship that makes polemic an obligatory part of scholarly work," they continue to assemble collections as a "promotion of pluralism" (Wertheimer 4). With cautious optimism, many scholars continue to unearth women and women's ways, searching for new understandings, developing varying rhetorical lenses that help us to further our knowledge and understanding of women in the history of rhetoric. Such examination is essential, since "history's representations of the past help construct gender for the present. Analyzing how that happens requires attention to the assumptions, practices and rhetoric of the discipline, to things either taken for granted or so outside customary practice that they are not usually a focus for historians' attention" (Scott 2).

While I share scholars' concerns about recuperating individual women and respect the need to proceed with questions, I nonetheless value that recuperation and welcome the lively discussion surrounding issues with regards to our tradition. In our fledgling attempts to provide some symmetry to our tradition after centuries of imbalance, can we have too much information about women? Can we examine too many alternative ways of defining rhetoric? If so, I am willing to risk that possibility. I welcome ongoing efforts to redress the inequity.

Although much early work has focused on the rediscovery of important women rhetoricians, the recovery has also sought new methods of defining rhetoric more appropriately. Molly Wertheimer sees minimal disagreement about disparate methods, since methods often overlap or lead one to the other. For example, even though Karlyn Kohrs Campbell's work is generally regarded as important for its recovery of women speakers, Campbell also sought to examine rhetoric through a new lens that could recognize and appreciate the courage, creativity, and rhetorical sophistication often hidden in those shadowy areas by a perspective that privileges masculine rhetoricians—a search for a "feminine style" (12–15). Unable to use a strong voice and forceful gestures, or even to make an argument without attention to specific criteria that might diminish charges against their femininity, women developed their own style of rhetoric. Campbell sought to help us understand and appreciate that style.

Linda Gordon lists four categories of feminist methodology for historical research: "1) defining what counts as evidence, 2) collecting evidence, 3) generalizing from specifics, and 4) drawing conclusions" (29). But she insists that only in the first category is there a "unique contribution" (29). Redefining what counts as evidence reshapes the way we understand history. But if recovery efforts have created controversy, changes in what we count as meaningful may create even more. Some recent scholarship attempts such a redefinition, but these efforts have brought questions and sharp criticism as well, especially such attempts with regards to accounts of Aspasia. Xin Liu Gale charges Cheryl Glenn with "abandonment of the traditional concern for truth and evidence" (366) and Susan Jarratt and Rory Ong of depending "heavily on interpretation and speculation" (373). Glenn deliberately contextualizes fragmentary information about Aspasia in order to read from a perspective outside the traditional interpretation of men, "reading it crookedly and telling it slant" in an effort to locate "a female rhetorical presence" (8). Jarratt and Ong "examine 'Aspasia' as a site of discourse," and

Jarratt claims validity for her use of factual claims to make "speculative leaps . . . to imagine the world differently from the way it has been handed down to us" (390, 391). Because these approaches differ markedly from traditional methods, they are accompanied by concerns and questions.

Bizzell sees these approaches, along with numerous others, most especially Jacqueline Jones Royster's recent scholarship, as bringing emotions to bear on feminist historical methodology.[1] Royster and others have acknowledged the affective in their methodology, explicitly identifying a component of the rhetorical tradition that has necessarily been present but gone unrecognized and unacknowledged. Such efforts demand that we concede the historically unseen traditions that have privileged some and denigrated others. We may continue to shape our tradition for some time before we come to agreement, or we may simply agree to disagree; meanwhile, contributions to what counts as evidence—as well as the questioning that provokes further examination and discussion about their merit—marks the vitality and validity surrounding scholarly activity in feminist historical scholarship in rhetoric today.

Amidst these exciting discussions and in the spirit of seeking an increased understanding of women and their presence and practices in our rhetorical heritage, I offer *Appropriate[ing] Dress*. I have sought to examine women and rhetoric primarily from the conspicuously gendered representation of women in the nineteenth-century United States to understand how bodies and dress helped to define the struggle for representation and power that is rhetoric. One component that contributes to our understanding and appreciation of women in the history of rhetoric is evidence crucial to their effectiveness but heretofore ignored because of its insignificance for men. Since rhetorical effectiveness has been determined historically according to standards appropriate to men—has privileged information and contexts that emphasize the strength and value of masculine qualities—the importance of clothing has been largely ignored, thereby diminishing our ability to recognize an essential component in the complex and often powerful rhetorical acumen on the part of women.

In recognizing the gendered nature of our history of rhetoric, Campbell aptly points out that women speakers "were constrained to be particularly creative because they faced barriers unknown to men" (8). Since many of the traditional tools of rhetoric were denied them, women found it necessary to consider techniques beyond masculine speakers' attention to argument and delivery. Campbell suggests further that "[r]hetorical invention is rarely originality of argument" (8) but a careful and creative choice and adaptation of materials. Although she does not identify dress as one of women speakers' strategies, I would suggest that clothing and appearance constituted a major component in the ethos women presented, an element taken for granted by men. That dress played such a major role in the depiction of women speakers, as noted by Fern, is especially significant. Women who assumed the public platform encountered ethical problems even before they spoke because dress "precede[s] verbal communication in establishing an individual's gendered identity as well as expectations for other types of behavior" and transmits information not readily translatable into words (Eicher and Roach-Higgins 17). Women speakers' visual appearance, marking gender (feminine) and intersecting with location (public and improper for women), might instantly preclude a credible ethos and negate efforts to employ logical and pathetic appeals.

Since gender has so clearly influenced the shaping of our tradition, references to the body have legitimized existing perceptions of gender or worked to change them. Because nineteenth-century women were so fully defined according to gender, and because gender was based largely upon dress and appearance, women understood the importance of clothing in negotiating the rigid power structure that permitted them little access to public attention. We have begun to discover paths that women marked out in order to better accommodate their corporeal forms. *Appropriate[ing] Dress* seeks to add to our understanding of how women (re)appropriated their own bodies, so often used against them, in order to challenge a hierarchy of power that strove to silence them.

I have concentrated primarily on women whose highly visible careers drew comments from audiences that are still available and for whom some trace of intention and regard for appearance and dress's impact on ethos is evident. These are primarily white middle-class women, living in the first half of the nineteenth century. Much more evidence is available in the second half of the century to help us understand how African American women made use of dress. I believe that all women speakers, because of the close relationship dress and appearance had with the construction of gendered identity and perceptions of character, were cognizant of its importance, even though some used it more successfully than others. Dress was important for white men as well, but they had less reason to attend closely to dress. Simply by donning the uniform apparel that signified their masculinity, they claimed a privileged status accommodated by the platform. This standing did not necessarily extend to black men because, while their dress announced their right to a public persona, complexion often qualified that right.

Negotiation of Gendered Images

When assuming a place uncustomary for women, such as the platform, women rhetors could not rely upon an "appropriate" dress, as none had been established. In addition, dress evoked immediate images of gender, an essential consideration for women speakers because of its strong association with place. Such locating of bodies according to visual presentation, in a specific place at a proper time, created a primary image that women speakers would work with and against throughout the century. The "woman question" and growing anxiety about changing roles heightened emphasis on appearance as a defining feature that ensured neat categories for the sexes, adding to the tension. Opposition to conspicuous change for women often necessitated subtle transfer of comforting images into places women sought. As they assumed the platform, the most successful women carefully negotiated expectations by highlighting some conventions as they broke others.

Given their breach of customary roles as they assumed powerful public positions, women found that ethical development was far more important for them than for men. It was even more important for black women, especially when speaking before white audiences. White middle-class women were expected to be more "moral" than men, and so their behavior was much more rigidly defined and restricted. Breaching precise expectations with regards to gender led to charges of immorality—a rupture in what had come to be socially authorized as the very essence of femininity. African American women, having been depicted as promiscuous and immoral by nature, faced an even greater ethical challenge.

Public speaking, coded masculine, did not of itself threaten social norms when men participated; for women, however, it was doubly problematic. Because gender was the defining feature for women, public success for women speakers was largely determined by their ability to negotiate gender constraints in a manner that allowed audiences to identify with them, to hear, and ultimately to consider and agree with both their role and their words. Women thus found it necessary, as they broke some cultural restrictions for their sex, to "yield to [the] audiences' opinions in other respects" (Burke 56). The careful negotiation between broken regulations and concessions to expectations defines the most successful women rhetors. The most typically manipulated component of presentation, because the most visible and dichotomous in terms of gender, was dress. The title for this book illustrates my belief that because dress for women already had an established and well-defined rhetoric, one especially important for ethical presentation, many women speakers readily appropriated and capitalized on that rhetoric.

Dress Makes the Woman

As women developed effective means of presenting themselves rhetorically, constructions of a natural gender showed evidence of fracture. Disruptions in both the expected appearance of the body and the space which that body had permission to occupy exposed the fabricated nature of gender by a constantly shifting play with images of woman's body, its gender, its place, and its performance. Such challenges to notions on which an entire culture was constructed engendered fear, of course, and subsequent reprisals against those "who fail[ed] to do their gender right" (Butler 140). As changes in women's appearance and location required new ways of reading women's bodies, critics resisted such readings by focusing on dress in their disparagement of women activists. Throughout the nineteenth century, opponents' rebukes and newspaper headlines read changes in women's traditional place primarily according to clothing and appearance.

Woman's gendered appearance, inscribed by an elaborately ornamented and detailed wardrobe, not only defined her femininity but also systematically and simultaneously distinguished her place. That is, the cut and detail of her dress, often accompanied by the specific style of her hair, signified her proper temporal location—the ballroom gown, lawn party dress, riding habit, walking dress, or morning wrapper—as well as social or class position. Fashion periodicals regularly recommended appropriate apparel according to time of day and site of attendance. The appropriately dressed woman "would need gowns for the morning hours, for afternoons at home, for visiting, for dinners, or for receptions and balls. Periods of mourning were long and called for rigid observance. . . . There were costumes for promenading and costumes for traveling" (Blum vi). Obviously, a rhetoric of dress was in place.

Largely because of such gendered images and customs, scholars often describe nineteenth-century women in relation to power, especially in terms of Foucault's "docile bodies," disciplined into a passive existence, specifically with regards to dress. Not unlike Foucault's ideal soldier, women could be readily recognized by dress. Similarly, their postures, defined both by clothing—corsets, tight lacing, numerous petticoats—and convention— a reticent and humble demeanor—further created an easily discernable image.[2]

But if dress became a means of control, a way of disciplining women, it also provided an effective means of resistance as many women used clothing and "feminine" style to escape the silence to which they had been relegated. In their efforts to project a positive ethos, women made dress speak for them.

Clothing not only allowed them a way to construct the image they would project. It also represented a manner of expression or a supplement to voice for a group restricted and discouraged from expressing itself publicly.

Its success as a disciplining force made clothing all the more effective as a tool for some nineteenth-century women speakers because of its alignment with the domestic arena. Constructed in its use comprehensively and from an early age, women acquired a comfort and facility with clothing that imparted both a sophisticated conscious knowledge and intuitive understanding of its powerful effect on the attitude of others. At the same time, dress's appearance of discipline was so comprehensive that critics were often slow in recognizing its possibilities for resistance.

To appreciate play with clothing and its relevance for issues of character and power for rhetors, it is important to understand the pervasive premises surrounding dress and place for women. Nineteenth-century culture strictly confined women to the domestic sphere. Women might leave the home for certain functions: Visiting in others' homes was acceptable, as was attendance at diversionary functions, such as balls. Among the lower classes, women might be employed outside their own homes; however, their association with domestication usually continued as limited employment pursuits most often reflected their accepted place: sewing, laundering clothes, or attending to details of everyday home life for the upper classes. Even women who worked in the mills usually reflected traditional conceptions of space for women, employed as they were in the manufacture of cloth or other items of apparel. While particular association with the domestic varied greatly for women according to class, nineteenth-century convention assumed a uniform location that all women should inhabit; those who took the public platform therefore found it necessary to contend with images that confined them to the domestic.

Historical Gendering of Dress

Whereas both men and women in previous centuries had dressed elaborately, or not, according to their class, in the nineteenth century emphasis on gender became exaggerated; women's clothing continued to be colorful and decorative whereas men's became increasingly somber, plain, and uniform. Although consistently ornate, women's clothing changed. For example, at the beginning of the century, women's fashions emphasized empire waist designs, a style that gathered fabric beneath the bust and permitted garments to flow loosely around the waist and hips. Midcentury saw women's assigned place in society increasingly challenged as reform efforts began to flourish. At this time, dress further exaggerated the differentiation in physical body. Women's dress increased focus on the waistline, often with narrow skirts of clinging materials accompanying low-cut bodices and exposed shoulders, or fuller skirts with elaborate petticoats, hoops, bustles, and crinolines, often gathered at the side and back to further define the corseted and laced midsection.

This most visual representation of gender and status has provoked critics to search for meaning behind the often elaborate means of display. Lawrence Langer notes that

> the differentiation in clothing between men and women arose from the male's desire to assert superiority over the female and to hold her to his service. This he accomplished through the ages by means of special clothing which hampered or handicapped the female in her movements. Then men prohibited one sex from wearing the clothing of the other, in order to maintain this difference. (31)

Excluding problematics of race, Langer also observes that the skin is an "equalitarian uniform that man has sought to negate in order to achieve superiority over others" (3).

Such speculation on the meaning behind the tradition of ornamentation and symbolism in women's dress has led scholars to view such intricate apparel as sinister with regard to women, especially during the Victorian period. Helene Roberts feels that clothing conventions contributed to making woman "the exquisite slave," often "willing to cashier the masochistic, submissive, and narcissistic role of women" (568–69). Langer and Roberts typify the dismay at clothing encumbrances endured by Victorian women. Indeed, scholars often focus on the patriarchal control inherent in dress dichotomies. Alison Lurie marks the gender inequities in nineteenth-century clothing, with women's clothing designed specifically to present women's frail immaturity through pale colors and fragile materials. Lurie claims that clothing helped to position women somewhere between children and angels, as "weak, timid, innocent creatures of sensitive nerves and easily alarmed modesty who could only be truly safe and happy under the protection of some man" (216).

Such condemnations of women's attire are common, and the nineteenth-century United States seems especially culpable given its dichotomous dress requirements. Colin McDowell sees that century as the "one above all others in which the gap between . . . standards expected of men and women yawned wide." In contrast to the "rectitude and reliability" in men's clothing, McDowell sees the "vanity and triviality" exemplified by women's "ever-changing and increasingly excessive fashions" as especially malevolent:

If an arbitrary decision is made that plainness and sobriety of dress are the prerequisites of the governing sex, and the other sex is encouraged, or even forced, into an obsessive preoccupation with decorative variations in dress, then that sex cannot pose a serious challenge to the hegemony of the governing sex. . . . This is what men did to women in the nineteenth century when they renounced decorative clothing and made it a plaything for the "ladies." They placed women on a pedestal, out of the way, to be admired and noticed only when men wished them to be, as decorative, even valuable, artistic acquisitions, but mute and irrelevant in terms of the real, masculine world beyond the dressmaker's establishment. (McDowell 52)

Such comments indicate how dress for women constructed an oppressive, structured place and image for women, but clothing did not simply define temporal location.

Dress, Appearance, and Social Position

Dress and appearance were already implicated in a hierarchy of power representing economic and social status. Standards of beauty and acceptability were based largely on notions of the ideal, or "true," woman. The degree to which women met expectations for this ideal often determined their rewards and punishments. Marriage to a kind, loving, and wealthy husband was generally considered the greatest reward. If unmarried, the ideal woman was young and virginal, humble and caring, cloistered and protected in the home of her father or other appropriate guardian. Later, as wife and mother, she became the nurturing and sheltered treasure in a man's home. The ideal woman knew when to be silent and spoke quietly when it was appropriate for her to speak. She had no need for income or employment as she was fully supported and protected by the man in her life.

Such ideas closely paralleled the feminine ideal, based on Euro-American, middle-class expectations. Femininity was defined by a petite frame, delicate facial features, small hands and feet, a tiny waist, white porcelain complexion, and silky long hair. Feminine features might be enhanced by grooming according to the current acceptable fashion. If constructions of the ideal woman and femininity heightened acceptance and status for some women, their very exclusive characteristics negated the feminine value of others, especially poor women and those of color.

Dress was highly implicated in social position as well. Clothing generally defined class for women, and the dress of *their* women reflected the status and power of men. That is, women of well-to-do men dressed elegantly and in fashions that demonstrated their leisurely status. As economist Thorstein Veblen points out, what passed as elegant apparel demonstrated "that it is contrived at every point to convey the impression that the wearer does not habitually put forth any useful effort" (170). "Elegant dress serves its purpose of elegance not only in that it is expensive, but also because it is the insignia of leisure. It not only shows that the wearer is able to consume a relatively large value, but it argues at the same time that he consumes without producing" (171).³

Possessiveness of status paralleled and encompassed ownership associated with both gender and class. Although most states had never officially instituted sumptuary laws, the Americas had, in fact, a long de facto history of such injunctions, and notions about such regulation permeated the culture. Popular New England literature often referenced earlier sumptuary laws. In Catharine Maria Sedgwick's early popular historical novel, *Hope Leslie,* Reverend Cotton announces a "sumptuary regulation" (165), and Everell Fletcher warns Sir Philip Gardner that the colony's sumptuary laws might "prove inconvenient" to Roslin (128). Similarly, Nathaniel Hawthorne suggests in *The Scarlet Letter* that Hester Prynne violated Puritan sumptuary expectations. Such references and inferences continued throughout much of the nineteenth century.

Possessiveness of status as exemplified in dress surfaced repeatedly. Some U.S. state laws denied slaves the right to wear clothing that appropriated the status of free whites, even when those clothes were deemed no longer adequate for white masters. Slaves were often criticized for having clothes "too good for any of [their] colour" (qtd. in White and White 17), and white slaveholders expressed concerns for "the way we indulge them in sinful finery," believing "We will be punished for it" (Chesnut 206).⁴

Dress was considered a proper means of keeping free blacks in their place as well. Some West Indian colonials had instituted laws that forbade "'gens de couleur,' the free women of color, to wear extravagant clothes surpassing those of the white women" (Raiskin 54, n. 7). Whites typically caricatured free blacks who presumed to feign a rank equal with them, complaining that they "aped the dress of their masters, long before they are cast off" (qtd. in White and White 114). And white middle-class women typically complained of the "inordinate development of negro women's love for dress" (Kearney 55). As White and White point out, "Whites' *physical* response to the sartorial strategies of blacks suggests that they clearly recognized, in the black adornment of the body, a highly political subtext of struggle, a determination to renegotiate the social contract" (128).

Such attitudes were not directed only at people of color. In New Orleans, Creoles regularly taunted Anglos with scornful ditties that referred to them as "rogues dressed in nankeen" to emphasize the English inelegance in style (Tallant 84). White women of the lower and working classes dressed differently from the upper classes. Distinctions were not readily violated, especially early in the century, because of the extravagant expense entailed in creating the upper classes' wardrobes. Many women could hardly afford cloth. Clothing was often "scavenged and/or handed down" (Boydston 37), and when cloth was available, only the upper classes could afford either expensive and ornate fabrics and ornamentations or the skilled work of seamstresses. Clothing was so dear that it served as currency, often "pawned overnight . . . to cover the rent until payday" (42). Despite early assumptions that a few years' work in the mills provided a lark for many young women, allowing them to indulge in fineries of dress, the majority of mill workers' wages helped to sustain workers' families. The increasing employment of immigrant workers in the mills after 1830 saw a class of workers even less able to indulge in expensive clothing.

However, economic factors provided only one component that delineated sharply between the image of the "lady" and women of lesser social class. As Gerda Lerner points out, in the proffered "formulation of values, lower-class women were simply ignored" (39). Periodicals presented appropriate dress for "ladies," and discourse about dress generally referred to dress of the middle and upper classes. Lower-class women who imitated "ladies" of the upper classes were held in disdain. "Although female servants wore clothes similar to those of their mistresses, there was no danger that one would be mistaken for the other. . . . Somber colors, poorer fabrics stripped of trimmings, along with a maid's or nurse's headdress would indicate the servant's station in society" (Blum vii). Such attitudes were often reflected in commentaries on dress, authorities insisting on clean and groomed workers. Pointing out "the effect of dress upon the character and condition of servants," author and editor Caroline Kirkland warned that "domestics sometimes act so earnestly upon this principle, that they end in erring on the side of too much attention to costume" (154). Issues of morality often played into notions of dress as well, and women were arrested and/or fined for wearing Mother Hubbard dresses or other clothing considered "inappropriate" ("Dress Reform in Chicago").[5] Dress clearly repeated definitions of race, class, gender, and morality, all closely associated with character.

When women began to speak publicly, rupturing expectations for women's place, opponents focused on the other primary definition of gender—dress—especially where white middle-class women were concerned. Nonetheless, to view women's dress and mobility only from a negative perspective denies the numerous strides women made assisted by dress, both in restructuring their place in society and in reconstructing their gendered image. Such a narrow perspective also belies women's ability to appropriate existing hegemonic constrictions on gender to further their own intentions. While cultural restrictions did create an often difficult terrain, many women deftly negotiated that territory in order to reimagine themselves in a world more conducive to their needs. This cultural negotiation was particularly important for women speakers. Yet, as women strove to create a positive public presence, other exaggerated dichotomies served to further complicate matters.

Gendered Notions of Rhetoric

Rhetorical style had historically been relegated masculine and feminine characteristics, with those attributes assigned the feminine presented in negative terms. Such representations followed throughout the western tradition of rhetoric, with abundant references in classical rhetoric, beginning perhaps with the description in Plato's *Gorgias* of self-adornments as "rascally, deceitful, ignoble, and illiberal nature [that] deceives men by forms and colors, polish and dress," neglecting truth, for example. Conceptions of the ideal rhetor continued to be presented in the form of the good *man*. Both Susan Jarratt and Miriam Brody have noted the long-standing association of the feminine with negative connotations in rhetoric. Brody has convincingly outlined a tradition of rhetoric that assumed a masculine rhetor, tracing gendered metaphors that equated good rhetoric with the masculine and poor rhetoric with the feminine or effete. In addition, school texts merged "heroic ideals of the older, manly warrior–civic statesman and the manly entrepreneur" (Brody 116), leaving little room for the womanly. Such inferences abounded in the nineteenth century.

This association of women with elaborate style and adornment in the nineteenth century was accompanied by strict notions of propriety that assigned women to the private, men to the public, creating further difficulties for the publicly active woman. Conventional wisdom held that "There is something profane in the public eye, and therefore . . . a well-bred woman should never . . . attract and fix it" (Kirkland 99). In the face of such customs, women had to negotiate expectations for a public, strong, and masculine mode of rhetoric. Those women who sought to become effective public persons found it necessary to mediate the tension created by traditional notions of valid rhetoric and conventional concepts of feminine appearance to manage the perilous gender dichotomy that immediately undermined women speakers' credibility. "Any woman who had the temerity to step forth upon the public platform to address a promiscuous assembly was considered by most people in nineteenth-century America to be without [virtue]"—an absolutely essential component for ethical appeal (O'Connor 134).

As women broke cultural restrictions by speaking publicly, other gendered norms came under increased scrutiny. Women "had to simultaneously turn down the level of the body to assume the subject position of man and also turn up the level of the body to reassure the [audience] that the body was aligned as a woman's body should be aligned socially within the matrix of reproduction and nurturing" (Smith 25). Problematic, then, were traditional requirements for "forceful" and effective public speaking because such customary expectations further removed women from their expected gendered role. Vocal exercises to permit powerful speech and practice in virile stance and gestures served notions of masculinity but undermined images of the feminine.

Opponents seized upon gendered notions of dress and physical appearance to criticize women speakers. Early in the century, they defined women participants in temperance meetings as Amazons, and scorned those "responsible" for them in terms of feminine dress: "The husbands and parents of these modern Amazons, should be arrayed in caps and aprons, and installed in their respective kitchens" ("We Are Glad"). Individual women also received reprimands associated with dress. Lewis Tappan impugned Maria Chapman by suggesting that she manipulated people as readily as women work with clothing: She "manages William Lloyd Garrison, Wendell Phillips, and Quincy as easily as she could untie a garter" (qtd. in Pease and Pease 29); historian George Bancroft described her "coterie" as "a squad of blue-stockings" (qtd. in Pease and Pease 39).

At midcentury, as a larger number of women became publicly active, meetings where women spoke were often announced with such headers as "Insurrection of Petticoats" and "Women's Scramble for the Breeches." Because many reformers in other causes also participated in dress reform, criticism often focused on the attire they wore in an effort to change traditional, constrictive clothing, especially on the most famous of reform dresses, the Bloomer. "Those who wore Bloomers were called 'Amazons,' 'nondescripts,' and 'brazen creatures'" ("Dress Reform and Moral Reform"). Headlines read "Petticoats and Pantiloons," "A Female in Breeches," and "A Female in Pantaloons."

By the final decades of the century, though, women speakers and women's mass organizational meetings became less a novelty. Still, much opposition to women's changing roles continued, and headlines often focused on women's dress, frequently referencing undergarments ("Corset-Strings and

Suffrage"; "The Corseted Crusade"; and "Politicians in Petticoats") or focused on women's bodies ("A Bustline Army of Crusaders"). Women who achieved success in professions usually reserved for men were so defined as well. When women began to attend law schools, for example, reports heralded "Petticoats at the Bar."

Critics whose purpose was to provoke fear of this new woman nearly always did so through dress metaphors. Dr. Henry Bellows asked, "Place woman unbonneted and unshawled before the public gaze and what becomes of her modesty and virtue?" (qtd. in Stanton et al. 245).[6] The question was obviously a rhetorical one. The answer often came in the form of headers that suggested public women's unprincipled and manipulatively alluring nature: "They flirt their flounces and caps on the platform." Even newspapers that assumed an "objective" position and avoided direct physical descriptions of women and their apparel seemed unable to resist focus on their bodies. When the American Woman Suffrage Association met in New York in May 1870, the *New York Times,* which delivered a precise enumeration of resolutions passed and speakers presented, reported that "Ladies of all shapes and sizes were present at an early hour" ("Woman Suffrage"). Having always identified women by body and appearance, reporters seemed unable to describe women in any other terms. Significantly, as reporters came to accept women speakers, they reported according to dress and appearance in order to reassure readers of speakers' honorable character and acceptable social position.

In addition, efforts to punish women by focusing on dress often undermined opponents' own effectiveness. Threats that women who broke gender rules should be "spanked" (Watterson 199) or would be left spinsters disclosed the material dimension to women's "protected" status as well as their marketability. Similarly, depictions of women speakers as bitter social outcasts seemed extreme. After the 1852 Woman's Rights Convention at Syracuse, for example, the *New York Herald* claimed,

> Some of them are old maids, whose personal charms were never very attractive, and who have been sadly slighted by the masculine gender in general; some of them women who have been badly mated, whose own temper, or their husband's, has made life anything but agreeable to them, and they are therefore down upon the whole of the opposite sex; some, having so much of the virago in their disposition, that nature appears to have made a mistake in their gender— mannish women, like hens that crow. ("The Woman's Rights Convention")

Such attacks, "animalizing" women and reducing them to their sex, are typical of efforts to demean women (Conboy et al. 84). However, such public reprimands further highlighted and promoted the public images of the reprobate "private" woman, normalizing readers' perceptions of women in a myriad of locations and suggesting the constructed nature of the boundaries critics were striving to maintain.

To add to a growing positive recognition, women's backgrounds and personalities became known nationally. As readers became familiar with women speakers through such newspapers as the *Lily* and the *Wyndham County Democrat* and as reporters and audiences experienced firsthand the personalities and appearances of these women, the obvious misrepresentation in such charges weakened credibility of opponents. In addition, the national and international attention some women achieved created a celebrity that drew audiences and promoted the more acceptable ethos that such star quality advances.

Perhaps most significantly, growing numbers of women who defied customary gender restraints contributed to a reconstructed image of gender simply by their appearance. Their insistence on associating with multiple places conferred legitimacy on a public role for women; their refusal to repeat the traditionally forged reflection of elaborately clothed and sheltered women helped to eliminate the showy and constrictive clothing that defined women as restricted, frail, and helpless, and also normalized images of a public woman.

Still, progress was slow, and advances were often treacherous. If one of the primary factors of persuasion was the speaker's ethos and the perceived ideal rhetor was "the good man speaking well," the gender of the speaker mattered. While character was important for men who would be public figures, that of women was much more closely scrutinized and with more critical presumptions. Most members of nineteenth-century audiences believed that "the expression of our dress is nearly as characteristic as that of our faces" (Kirkland 157); therefore, appearance played a great role in determining perceptions about character and could wield powerfully effective rhetoric for women. Women thus assumed a fastidious balancing act that negotiated multiple gendered presentations within a multitude of locations.

1

Friendly Dress: A Disciplined Use

The very garments of a Quaker seem incapable of receiving soil; and cleanliness in them to be something more than the absence of its contrary. Every Quakeress is a lily; and when they come up in bands to their Whitsun conferences, whitening the easterly streets of the metropolis, they show like troops of the Shining Ones.
—Charles Lamb, "A Quaker's Meeting"

*E*arly women speakers who so blatantly broke conventional strictures against woman's private place immediately found their moral character questioned. "[U]nless and until they could be acceptable as individuals of character even as they spoke in public, there was little need to establish anything else about themselves" (O'Connor 137). Lillian O'Connor thus notes early women speakers' appeals "that they were doing God's work, and [that] they displayed knowledge of the . . . Bible" (139). However, by including references to biblical texts and to their own efforts on behalf of "God's work," women deliberately supplemented such allusions to their moral worth with visual detail that helped to prepare the hearer before their first words were spoken.

In the early nineteenth century, most of the best-known and most effective women speakers wore Quaker attire.[1] Such association served to suggest a religious sincerity on the part of the speaker. Since purity was a prerequisite for credibility and respectability for nineteenth-century women, and convention held that purity was impossible for women except in the domestic sphere, a visual image that evoked sentiments of morality and purity prepared an audience better than any other dress could have to seriously consider the speaker. At a time when the "notorious" woman's rights advocate Frances Wright was assailed for "immodest" dress and ideas when speaking in public, subsequent speakers clothed themselves in the religiously significant dress and bonnet, thwarting critics who equated women's public speaking with decadent morals, prostitution, and brazenness.

Few women at this time dared to expose themselves to the gaze and disdain of a "respectable" society that insisted on a specific private place for women, at least for white women of certain classes. Women's activities outside the home were restricted primarily to church and benevolent societies, and "most of the women who worked in them gave no public speeches, wrote no political pamphlets, and did not see their . . . activities as challenging the traditions of male authority and female domesticity" (Sánchez-Eppler 23). By the 1830s, women were joining temperance and abolition associations in large numbers, often forming their own societies. But whether a part of the principal men's organizations or the separately formed women's groups, their role was essentially supporting the men. The normalized image of women permitted no public exposure or voice. Defying such roles, Wright began speaking publicly in 1828. Her views concerning the emancipation of women and slaves, religion, and education reform made her a pariah. Unwilling or unable to negotiate intersecting elements of appearance, Wright challenged norms for women's image and emphasized the radical change of place she undertook. She became an easy target for proponents of slavery and those opposed to women's public efforts in general, both of whom denounced her as a threat to moral and religious ideals.

The Red Harlot of Infidelity

Wright's genteel Scottish heritage and her close relationships with Jeremy Bentham[2] and the much admired General Lafayette enhanced her position as a public speaker. However, her radical appearance and extreme stance on many issues diminished benefits she gained from her background and associations. Women's closely regulated appearance and culturally controlled position supported notions of Wright's deviancy. Critics called Wright "masculine" and "unsexed," nearly always focusing on her dress or general appearance when attacking her. The tall, willowy Wright wore her naturally curly hair cropped short, challenging a major cultural stricture that separated women from men according to the length and style of hair. Opponents spotlighted gender and charged Wright with being less than a woman, often coupling masculine and feminine terms in ascribing identity to her. She regularly faced opposition that labeled her a "petticoated politician" or a "lady-man" (Eckhardt 224) or even "the great Red Harlot of Infidelity" (Rossing 102). Critics thus capitalized on the fear and anxiety surrounding gendered deviations from the norm.

Opponents focused on other aspects of her appearance as well. At times her dress consisted of Turkish trousers beneath a long-sleeved, knee-length tunic of fine material, bound at the waist by a flowing sash (see fig. 1.1). This dress, used at the New Harmony, Indiana, experimental socialistic commune with which Wright had been associated, had been designed for comfort and modesty (Lane 3), but opponents quickly charged it with in-

Fig. 1.1. Frances Wright in New Harmony dress. Courtesy of the Library of Congress.

delicacy. In the nineteenth century, "women glided or swept across the floor, since in polite discourse they had no legs" (Lurie 217–18). Wright broke such conventions by publicly demonstrating, through trousers, that women did, in fact, have legs.[3] The radical departure from traditional dress focused additional attention on Wright's body, which was already a spectacle because of her abandoning woman's assigned sphere. Even when she dressed more traditionally, critics reproached her. The *New York Daily Express* described her 1838 New York appearance as follows:

> She was dressed in white—with an open bosom, as if habited for a ball room, and with the exception of the usual share of legs exhibited by a Lecompte, or a Celeste, her performances would have answered well enough for an employ on some Theatrical Boards, at fifty cents a night, instead of six pence a head. ("Fanny Wright's Sunday Theatre")

Uncomfortable with Wright's appropriation of the platform, this reporter tried to categorize her according to woman's traditional place; her dress might fit her for only two places outside the domestic: the ballroom or the theater. After discussing the tremendous noise, applause, and calls and hisses from rowdies, the reporter again drew attention to Wright's physique: "Fanny at last put forth her bony finger, and with all the power of one of the Witches in Macbeth, stopt the boiling of the popular cauldron" (2).

Wright was also depicted in drawings. An 1838 political broadside depicted her in a low cut, albeit traditional, dress with her skirt drawn up to expose her leg nearly to the knee (see fig. 1.2). Such attention to Wright's appearance, and the accompanying association with sorcery and lewdness, portends a strategy that would become typical of nineteenth-century opposition to women speakers. As women began to join reform organizations, blurring accepted gender dichotomies, most language seemed inadequate to address notions of gender in other than binary terms or to perceive women except in relation to the corporeal. With place clearly demarcated for the sexes, women who crossed borders were charged with assuming features typically assigned to the "opposite" place or, as with witches, a woman's leaving the home associated her with "unnatural" bodies. Wright's sporting of radical attire, or even that appropriate for ballrooms, allowed for little play with images. Her appearance was read in relation to places traditionally assigned to women.

Critics readily associated Wright's nonconformity in dress with her revolutionary ideas. In addition to her opposition to slavery, Wright argued that women were men's equals and deserved equivalent roles in public life. Even more threatening to established institutions, Wright criticized organized

Fig. 1.2. Broadside portraying Frances Wright. Courtesy of the Library of Congress.

religion as a divisive panderer to power and spoke publicly about the value of sexual passion. In the early nineteenth century, when goodness and morality were most often equated with religious advocacy and women's place in the home was aligned with religious and moral guardianship, Wright's questioning of organized religion provided an easy mark for opponents, who accused her of attempting to destroy religion and charged that she was in favor of free love, or sexual intimacy outside marriage. In challenging so many established institutions and notions about woman's place, Wright was certain to meet with ridicule and opposition.

Although newspapers generally tendered the most vocal and obvious criticism, one of Wright's harshest critics was a woman, Catharine Beecher:

Who can look without disgust and abhorrence upon such an one as Fanny Wright, with her great masculine person, her loud voice, her untasteful attire, going about unprotected, and feeling no need of protection, mingling with men in stormy debate, and standing up with bare-faced impudence, to lecture to a public assembly. . . . There she stands, with brazen front and brawny arms, attacking the safeguards of all that is venerable and sacred in religion, all that is safe and wise in law, all that is pure and lovely in domestic virtue. (*Letters on the Difficulties of Religion* 23)

Beecher concisely addressed nearly all complaints against Wright in one paragraph. Like other critics, she filtered Wright's political stance through appearance, equating Wright's radical ideas with her body and attire. She followed the lead of critics who labeled any deviation from the norm for women as masculine and immoral. According to Beecher, a woman who usurped man's place on the platform assumed the masculine physical characteristics belonging to that place. Just as Wright's words evinced her defiance of social conventions, her dress further revealed her lack of moral discipline. Such criticism gave warning to women who might presume to speak openly—already breaking conventions for publicly silent women—that they would be examined according to every stricture and expectation by which the ideal woman was measured—by size, by musculature, by voice, by attire—all the facets that determined their "womanliness." In "abandoning" her assigned place, she forfeited the privilege of a pretended unawareness of physical details given "respectable" women.

Such attacks on Wright's person served to diminish her ethical acceptance, as did her irreverence toward organized religion, which created her most consistent opposition, with critics denouncing the "trashy philosophy" that confirmed her "detestation of the ministers of the Christian religion" ("For the Evening Post" 2). "Oh tempora, oh mores!" exclaimed one writer. "Here then we have in the city of New York, the prostitution of the female sex, the denial of the immortality of the soul, and the disbelief in the existence of an universal Creator" (2).

Such deviance from conventional expectations encouraged claims about the relationship between women's place and women's morality, often encoded in dress, and seemingly justified open threats of violence. When young men disrupted Wright's lectures with "thumpings, hisses, and a volley of expressions of the most vulgar and indecent kind," reporters justified police refusal to take action, calling the lecture a "den of Infidelity" ("For the Evening Post" 2). And Wright was also blamed for insults "offered to ladies and young unprotected females in the middle of the day" ("To Mr. Justice Wyman" 2) by gangs of young men. One writer suggested that "if our females think proper to countenance Miss Wright, by their presence at her licentious and demoralizing lectures," they should not be surprised to see the "principles there inculcated acted out in our public streets." The editor concurred: "What modest woman who respects herself or her sex or has a proper regard for decency and decorum, will again be seen entering the doors of what she calls her lecture room?" ("To the Editor" 2).

Apparently few "modest" women dared associate themselves with Wright's speeches. Women's organizations that would subsequently support women speakers remained silent. Elizabeth Oakes Smith later remembered that while she "saw nothing out of the way in [Wright's] extending her audience from the parlor to the forum" (Wyman *Selections* 83), others were not so accepting. Smith's family and friends opposed her attending a Wright lecture, and when Smith persevered, she found herself unlike the rest of the audience:

> The appointed hour had already arrived, and slowly, men, one after another, sauntered in—several women also, some with babes in their arms, and all bringing an atrocious odor of tobacco, whiskey, and damp clothing. At length there might have been fifty persons, not more, present, and these began to shuffle and call for the speaker. It was all so much more gross and noisy than anything I had ever encountered where a woman was concerned, that I grew quite distressed, and the bad atmosphere nearly made me faint. (84)

Opponents continued to associate women's public activity with the demise of morality and organized religion, seeing it as an attack on venerable institutions that served to order and maintain proper places. Nearly a decade after Frances Wright's questioning of religious organizations, the *New England Spectator* persisted in claiming that the Female Anti-Slavery Society demonstrated "a labored attack on the free Church and on the ministry, . . . evidently designed, as are some other recent movements, to make the anti-slavery organization an instrument to undermine and overthrow orthodoxy" ("Female Anti-Slavery Society"). Frances Wright made such an impression on her society that negative references to her are found well into the century. For example, in commenting on the proliferation of woman's rights conventions in 1848, the Philadelphia *Public Ledger and Daily Transcript* assured its readers that Philadelphia women were unlike those participating in such gatherings, that they preferred tending babies and objected to "a Fanny Wright for Mayor" ("The Women of Philadelphia"). Similarly, in 1851, when the *Boston Post* criticized dress reformers, the *Home Journal* suggested that instead of criticizing those reformers, the *Post* "should chatechise some Fanny Wright, or other strong-minded Fanny" rather than reprimand the admirable women working for more appropriate change ("Approaching Change in Ladies' Dress").

Frances Wright successfully thrust a new image of woman upon a public deeply committed to standardized binary gender roles; however, her radical appearance and public disdain for religion contributed to the further normalizing of the gendered culture. Her refusal to negotiate any of the expected gender roles made identification with her too frightening for most women. As Susan Bordo suggests, "No matter how exciting the destabilizing potential of texts, bodily or otherwise, whether those texts are subversive or recuperative or both or neither cannot be determined in abstraction from actual social practice" (294). Most women rejected all association with Wright and readily accepted the norm as preferable to Wright's presentation. "They want[ed], understandably, to be able to pursue happiness on the terms of the culture they live[d] in" (296). Succeeding women speakers deliberately sought to capture the interest and imagination of other women in order to successfully relate their messages and to bring about change for women. The most successful were sensitive to the "terms of the culture" in which their audience lived.

A Rhetorical Reassurance

Although women speakers who followed Wright experienced similar harsh criticism and opposition, their choice of dress deflected the focus on body and appearance that allowed critics to summarily dismiss Wright. Keenly aware of attacks that associated Wright with degeneracy, subsequent women speakers carefully constructed reassuring images that offered positive associations with their assigned place. For most, this meant strengthening their association with established religion and morality by foregrounding their Quaker dress. Their assumption of Quaker attire, which "loyally repeated" cultural expectations for dress, helped to mollify audiences at the same time that their use of space confounded expectations. Their diaries and letters make numerous references to Wright, primarily noting organizers' fears of women speaking at meetings lest they be called "Fanny Wright meetings" or be identified with immorality.[4]

Others' diaries attest to the strong reactions to the two modes of presentation. For example, Susan Cooper, wife of James Fenimore Cooper, writes in early 1831 of two women she met at one of Lafayette's soirées. Frances Wright, Cooper writes, had a face that "looks now like that of an old Bottle bruiser—and I do not know which is the most disgusting, her Appearance or her Doctrines." In contrast, Cooper takes note of the converted Quaker, Mrs. Opie (see fig. 1.3), whose "plain gauze Cap, and simple Dress, make her appearance very striking among the gay colours, and Feathers, and flowers at Paris" (Cooper 4–5).[5] Cooper writes fondly that their initial meeting with Mrs. Opie led to further pleasant visits. Cooper's reaction underscores how closely dress and appearance were related with character in early-nineteenth-century America. Opie was herself an avid reformer who would later attend the 1840 World Anti-Slavery Convention at which Elizabeth Cady

Stanton met Lucretia Mott. However, Opie's presentation of self, radically different from Wright's, helped to make Cooper receptive to her.

Such reverent attitudes influenced future women speakers as well. Stanton recalled that when she met Mott,

> I had always regarded a Quaker woman, as one does a Sister of Charity, as being above ordinary mortals, ready to be translated at any moment. I had never spoken to one before, nor been near enough to touch the hem of a garment. Mrs. Mott was to me an entire new revelation of womanhood. I sought every opportunity to be at her side, and continually plied her with questions. (Stanton et al. 420)

Similarly, Mary A. Livermore "ran away from school" when sixteen to hear Angelina Grimké speak before the Massachusetts legislature. Livermore "describes with great vividness the spiritual power that Miss Grimké exer-

Fig. 1.3. Amelia Opie, frontispiece for Cecilia Lucy Brightwell's *Memorials of the Life of Amelia Opie,* 1854. Inscription reads "Engraved by P. Lightfoot from a Medallion done in Paris by David."

cised over her audience—her frail figure and Quaker garb—her diffidence as she began to speak" (Burleigh 232).

While Stanton's and Livermore's appreciations of Quaker attire are somewhat specific to the wearer, positive testaments on Quaker dress in general abound. The quotation from Charles Lamb in the epigraph for this chapter represents one such perspective. Another significant viewpoint is that of Caroline Kirkland, an influential American writer and editor. In her 1850 series on dress that appeared in *Sartain's* fashion magazine, Kirkland notes, "Every one is charmed with this dress in its perfection: we never hear any one say it is not beautiful." Kirkland tells of

> a Friend who, without the least ostentation, refrained from wearing anything that had been dyed, preferring garments of the natural colour, as being the extreme of simplicity. The world might laugh at such a twilight-gray as this combination of soft browns produced, but the painter would have found in it something congenial to his eye, and a peculiar value in the purity with which it set off a fresh, ruddy complexion and silver hair. (101–2)

Even contemporary rhetorics inadvertently helped to promote positive notions of Quaker dress for women. In his 1808 *Letters on Literature, Taste, and Composition, Addressed to His Son,* George Gregory included in his advice the following perceptions of dress: "The style of an orator or declaimer may be compared to the full dress of a modern lady of taste and fashion; that of the philosopher should have all the neatness of a young and beautiful quaker" (qtd. in Brody 224 n. 5).[6]

Women speakers in Quaker dress effectively transferred reassuring images associated with another place and quelled opponents who questioned both their modesty and religious sincerity. Wright's dress, connoting specific locations, had allowed for little play with intersecting impressions. Religiously associated dress, on the other hand, permitted a wider range for polyvalent images. Specifically, Quaker style did not differentiate according to situations, as did traditional middle-class attire. So, although appearing in a public forum, the simple dress nonetheless evoked images of both the domestic and religious. In addition, the association of religious dress primarily with "men of the cloth" conferred an ethical authority onto the women speakers who wore it. Quaker dress could be "caught in the ambiguity of an actualization . . . dependent upon many different conventions, situated as the act of a present (or of a time) . . . [with] none of the univocity or stability of a 'proper'" (de Certeau 117). The play of images confounded those who would direct attacks at the body and appearance. Cooper's description of Opie, for example, demonstrates a positive impression associated with appearance, her primary reference being in opposition to specifics of conventional dress.

Quaker dress allowed for a play of various positive images as well. By clothing themselves in the simple dress, speakers wrapped themselves in the religious and social significance that accompanied the dress and signified their religious and moral relation to woman's traditional place. In fact, the issues of women's speaking, woman's rights, and dress became so closely associated that critics often connected woman's rights with Quakerism. For example, A. F. Williams, in opposing women's speaking at antislavery meetings, insisted he and other abolitionists had intended "to have nothing to say in anti-slavery meetings upon the 'woman question, alias Quakerism'; but it was found that those who favored that sect were determined to press it upon us, and that practically" ("Letter from A. F. Williams"). Such images placed these women in direct opposition to Frances Wright's disavowal of traditional orthodox positions because of their immediate association with Christianity. Rather than the negative impression of a Fanny Wright, the repeated public acknowledgment of the speakers' Quaker ties conferred a measure of respectability.

Notions of appearance and careful attention to costume intersected with other concepts about woman's place to undercut the sense of violation engendered by a woman's public speaking. As Abby Kelley noted, "The women in the [antislavery] society only asked the liberty to act according to their sense of duty" ("The Spirit of Slavery"), adapting responsibilities associated with the home and church to the platform. Justifications related to religion and duty allowed other women to feel comfortable in associating with and defending women speakers. Numerous women's antislavery groups promoted Sarah and Angelina Grimké's speaking tour of 1838 (see figs. 1.4 and 1.5). The Boston Female Anti-Slavery Society noted the sisters' eminent qualifications based on their "elevated and christian point of view" ("To Female Anti-Slavery Societies"). And the *Emancipator* defended their addressing promiscuous audiences by acknowledging their Quaker ties. Noting that they "do not go out as agents of the American Anti-Slavery Society," the newspaper insisted that if they did, the Society's nonsectarian policy "appeals to all to plead the cause of the slaves each in its own way." The *Emancipator* also did "not see how members of other sects could object to it any more justly than to admitting Friends as members" ("The Misses Grimké"). By such an argument, the *Emancipator* highlighted the Grimkés' religious connection, making clear to any reader that the sisters were members and supporters of organized religion.

Such association offered comfort and often served to moderate negative attitudes toward women speakers in the early part of the century. Some speakers who wore the distinctive apparel chose the dress out of commitment to the Society of Friends, often with little apparent conscious sense of its rhetorical effectiveness. Lucretia Mott was born into the Quaker religion and, despite ongoing conflict with her community, continued her membership in the Society of Friends throughout her life. "Though she always dressed in quaker costume," according to Elizabeth Cady Stanton, even Mott "attached no special significance to it as a means of grace" (Stanton et al. 424).

Numerous Quaker women, such as Abby Kelley Foster and Amy Post, who became publicly active, denounced or were themselves disowned by

Fig. 1.4. Angelina Grimké. Courtesy of the Library of Congress.

the Friends yet continued to wear the dress publicly when it served their needs. The South Carolina Grimkés, who converted only for a short time, continued to make use of the distinctive dress associated with the Society of Friends after their commitment to the religious group had lapsed, unwilling to relinquish the rhetorical advantage and safe social image that such dress afforded them. According to Angelina's husband, Theodore Weld, from the beginning of her "conversion," even among the Quakers in Philadelphia Angelina "would not wear an article of dress which caused her physical inconvenience, though it might be dictated by the universal usage of 'Friends'" (Stanton et al. 404). She often departed from Quaker rules of dress. "For this departure from usage, she was admonished," but the sisters' refusal to accept all the rules of dress was "regarded as quiet protests

Fig. 1.5. Sarah Grimké. Courtesy of the Library of Congress.

against some of the settled customs of the Society." On the other hand, the sisters' often conscious use of dress is apparent. The dress signified both religious sincerity and feminine stance on the part of all Quakers because of their opposition to violence and support of the weak. Such association lessened the masculine perception associated with their public speaking and allowed closer identity with and support of the sisters' position by many who had distanced themselves from Wright. Taken together, these women speakers who wore Quaker dress serve as examples of the shifting degrees of consciousness to which women used dress and appearance to "discipline" audiences and augment their own rhetorical effectiveness.

Quaker Maids: Pretty, Feminine, and Moral

Just as Frances Wright had been identified by appearance, the Quaker style provided the easiest and most prominent distinguishing identification for women speakers who wore it. But focus on Quaker dress differed radically from earlier attacks. James Russell Lowell helped to immortalize Abby Kelley's Quaker appearance, calling her a "simple Quaker maid," a "Judith turned Quakeress," in "modest dress" ("Hudibrastic Sketches"). The press noted Kelley's dress and overall appearance as well. For example, the *Bay State Democrat* reported her speech at the January 1842 Massachusetts Anti-Slavery Society in Boston as follows:

> A lady next appeared in the Speaker's chair, with a rich but plain Quaker dress, her dark hair smoothed placidly down on her fair cheek which glowed with the carnation's own deep hue, with beautifully curved lip, and full melting eye, and open brow of alabaster—the celebrated Abby Kelley—who with her sweetly melodious yet trumpet tones, poured forth her woman's soul in depicting the wrongs of the colored man. ("From the Bay State Democrat")

The *Democrat,* like most reporting on Kelley, focused on her appearance, initially identifying her by her Quaker dress and style. Such affiliation tended to temper subsequent comments. The positive portrait, while focusing on Kelley's appearance, contrasts sharply with depictions of Wright. Frederick Douglass attributed much of Kelley's success as an abolitionist speaker to her "youth and simple Quaker beauty" (Sterling 142). So strong was her association with the dress that even late-twentieth-century writers so identify her. Her biographer, Dorothy Sterling, refers to her as the "comely young woman in Quaker dress" (13), for example, and "Demurely dressed in Quaker Gray" (1). Although some of the positive reporting might be accounted for by Kelley's attractive features, which associated her with feminine ideals of beauty and dress, affiliating her with the Society of Friends undeniably helped make audiences receptive.

Angelina Grimké, too, was often characterized according to Quaker dress. The *Detroit Morning Post,* for example, in reporting on Grimké's appearance before a Massachusetts legislative committee, identified her as "a pretty quakeress from the south" ("A. E. Grimké"). Although both Grimkés protested that their public profiles should not be attributed to their Quaker religion, numerous supporters used just such a defense, and the Grimkés, despite their protest, repeatedly drew attention to their association with the Society of Friends.

Angelina Grimké became involved with the Quakers after joining her sister Sarah in Philadelphia. Sarah had already begun dressing as a Quaker, and eventually Angelina assumed the dress as well. Angelina immediately began commanding public attention, first by writing letters on political matters and then by public speaking. As their notoriety increased, the sisters' association with the Society of Friends became strained. By 1836 Sarah considered her Quaker ties severed but continued to wear the dress. In 1838, the Philadelphia Quakers officially expelled both sisters, Angelina for marrying Theodore Weld, a non-Quaker, and Sarah for attending their wedding. Sarah increased the hostility by writing a treatise entitled "Letter on the Subject of Prejudice Against Colour Amongst the Society of Friends in the United States."[7] Yet the sisters continued to wear the Quaker dress because they obviously understood the benefit they gleaned from such connections.

Theodore Weld often chided the Grimkés for their Quaker affectations. He scoffed at their "tight crimped caps, seven by nine bonnets, or that impenetrable drab that defieth utterly all amalgamation of color" (Barnes and Dumond 411). And he scolded Angelina for her meticulous detail to dress, suggesting that she was "in great danger of making a little God out of your caps and dull color" and worried that making "a certain shade of color . . . or arrangement of seams and angles [a] religion and principle" made them "*slaves* instead of rulers" (Barnes and Dumond 508). Weld's likening abolitionist women to slaves with regard to their dress suggests his sense of the disciplining power inherent in clothing. But the sisters, aware of their own appropriation of that power, refused to discard the dress.

Although Quaker attire ostensibly reflected the Friends' lack of concern with dress, women speakers, to varying degrees, took interest in dress and were cognizant of its power. Margaret Hope Bacon claims Kelley's "one vanity was her wardrobe" (*I Speak* 40), and she writes of Kelley's great sadness in selling some of the most expensive items in her wardrobe to allow her to further her work on behalf of slaves. Kelley writes in detail about dress—choosing capes to conceal daughter Alla's narrow chest, and discussing colors and various ornamental details of dress with Alla as she grew older.

The Grimké sisters seem to have been even more cognizant of the rhetorical impact of dress. They write about dress repeatedly in their diaries and letters. For example, Angelina—who apparently loved being the center of attention—comments often in her diary about the notice her Quaker dress affords her. She tells of a young man who uses her Quaker bonnet to make her acquaintance, bowing and asking for a Quaker cap because he has promised one to his sister (Lumkin 65). The incident allows the two to enter into light discussion.

Angelina also writes of "sailing down King Street" in her hometown Charleston, South Carolina, "among the gay & fashionable" (Lumkin 40) encased in prim Quaker garments. Angelina had previously dressed in an expensive, elegant style befitting the daughter of a wealthy and influential plantation owner. The simple Quaker dress would have contrasted sharply with her previous dress, and with the dress of other young women in town, in its repudiation of the numerous petticoats and extravagant ornamental embellishments typical of "fashionable" young southern women. In its unconventionality, the Quaker dress no doubt attracted much more attention than her expensive traditional clothing would have. In addition, the expensive clothing associated her with her plantation owner (slaveholding) background. In disposing of such dress and assuming Quaker clothing, she became more clearly associated with the slave population on whose behalf she spoke. Her acute sense of rhetorical presentation was evident even in the discarding of her elaborate clothing. Angelina writes of gathering her veils, laces, flounces, and trimmings from her hats and bringing them to Sarah, who called them "superfluities of naughtiness" and stuffed a cushion with them (Lumkin 31).

Celia Burleigh notes the singularity of the sisters' participation in Sunday morning services that drew further attention in Charleston:

> [W]hen the family left in carriages for St. Paul's, the fashionable and orthodox church, the sisters, clad in their sober attire, took their way on foot through the streets to the little Friends' meeting-house. A touch of the humorous lighted up these Sunday devotions. Besides themselves, there were but two Quakers in Charleston, a couple of old men who for years had been bitter enemies. After sitting in silence for an hour, the two old men would rise, each in turn shake hands with the sisters, and, loftily ignoring each other, stalk out of the building by opposite doors. (232)

In one of her famous "Letters on the Equality of the Sexes," published in the *Liberator* in 1838, Sarah Grimké states that "Christianity struck at the root of all sin, and consequently we find the early Christians could not fight or swear, or wear costly clothing." She notes the gradual intervention of pagan customs that led to concern again with elaborate dress. Grimké calls attention to her own Quaker dress by disavowing any wish that a uniform dress be adopted "lest anyone may suppose [that] from my being a Quaker" ("Dress of Women" 16). Grimké also claims that God called special attention to dress through his prophet Isaiah, who insisted that Jewish women not "adorn themselves with broidered hair, or gold, or pearls, or costly array" (Isaiah 3.16). She finishes by asking her audience to imagine their impressions on seeing ministers of the gospel arrayed with "ear-rings dangling from their ears, glittering rings on their fingers, and a wreath of artificial flowers on their brow, and the rest of their apparel in keeping." While Grimké was certainly earnest in her appeal for simpler attire for women, her focus on dress and its connection with religion and ministers inescapably associated her with orthodox piety and authority, furthering her own effectiveness. Her visualizing of trinketed ministers, and the contrast such an image produced to the serious reception clergy expected and attained in their somber, plain dress, demonstrates also her understanding of the rhetorical impact of clothing and appearance.

Angelina Grimké alluded to clothing as well in her address before the Massachusetts legislature. Drawing a parallel between Queen Esther's appeal that "achieved the salvation of millions of her race from the edge of the sword" and her own appeal on behalf of women, Angelina nonetheless drew distinct differences between her own simple appearance, associated with purity, and the royal, sensuous dress of Esther. "The Queen of Persia . . . trained as she had been in the secret abominations of an oriental harem" reached the king through sensual appetites. "Hence we find her arrayed in royal apparel" attempting to influence "through personal charms, and sensual gratification" ("Angelina E. Grimké" 35).

Claiming a similar mission, Grimké expresses gratitude "that we live in an age of the world too enlightened and too moral to admit of the adoption of the same means to obtain as holy an end." Presenting a petition with the signatures of 20,000 Massachusetts women requesting an end to slavery in the District of Columbia, she flatters her audience: She will not insult the legislators "by arraying my person in gold, and silver, and costly apparel" because they "cannot be reached but through the loftier sentiments of the intellectual and moral feelings" ("Angelina E. Grimké" 35).

Both Grimkés, in focusing explicitly on dress, indirectly drew attention to their own attire, which subsequently added to their appeal. And repeated allusions to biblical dress permitted them to associate themselves firmly within a godly tradition. It also allowed them to justify their own public activity by likening it to that of loved heroic women of the Bible. Furthermore, the change to Quaker attire served numerous other purposes in their extensive travels as public speakers, and they acknowledged the benefits. First, the cumbersome trunks and attendants necessary for typical middle-class women travelers would have made frequent travel extremely difficult. In addition, women usually did not travel alone because of assumptions about and dangers to "unprotected women." But the sisters did travel alone to speaking engagements, and Angelina comments on their nunlike appearance and the protection it affords them (Lumkin 63). But, perhaps of greatest importance, the identity associated with the religious Quakers through costume offered some measure of protection from and credibility with audiences. The usual aspersions cast at the characters of women who dared to seek public attention were somewhat assuaged because of their religiously significant clothing.

Taking Quaker Women Seriously

In assuming the simple dress of the Quakers, these women were able to divert attention from their bodies and ensure some consideration for their cause. Whether they spoke on behalf of slaves or women, critics were far more likely to respond seriously to their words. Ministers had summarily dismissed Wright, focusing criticism on her bodily form, but they responded publicly and with serious attention to the Grimkés. Although not identifying them by name, the Congregational Ministers of Massachusetts, in their now famous "Pastoral Letter," devoted a systematic rebuttal to the demands for greater rights for women, especially those made by the Grimkés. Similarly, Catharine Beecher addressed Angelina Grimké in *An Essay on Slavery and Abolitionism with Reference to the Duty of American Females.* The controversies, of course, provided attention and significance to the Grimkés, as well as a public spotlight on Beecher, who was arguing against just such visibility on the part of women. While opposition to the Grimkés was nearly as great as that for Frances Wright, opponents were far more likely to take them seriously and less likely to address attention to their bodies, in part because their appearance associated them with morality. Additionally, Wright's adversaries had attacked her personal character with charges of lewdness; opponents of Quaker women objected most commonly to the fact of their speaking publicly.

Both Kelley and the Grimkés felt no compunction in discontinuing the religious dress when the Quaker attire no longer served their political and rhetorical purposes. All three later adopted the Bloomer costume. Abby writes to her husband, Stephen, of working in her garden, climbing ladders to gather fruit from trees, attired in a Bloomer, and notes her impatience at the attention the costume draws (Sterling 297). The Grimkés displayed the Bloomer more publicly. They wore it at Belleville, New Jersey, where they moved in 1840. Henry David Thoreau writes of an 1856 visit to Eagleswood, where the Welds and Grimké were operating a boarding school. Thoreau notes seeing "Angelina Weld in extreme Bloomer costume, which you might call remarkable" (Thomas 233). Kelley also writes of visiting the school in Eagleswood. Both Angelina Grimké Weld and Sarah Grimké were attired in Bloomer costume for teaching (Sterling 297). The change represents a major shift in how the women presented themselves, from Quaker dress, with its implications of moral and religious fervor, to the Bloomer, connoting defiance and suggesting a more worldly activity for women. The new dress marked them as prepared to defy social customs of dress/place in the interest of a greater freedom for women, rather than presenting the orthodox Christian image they had cultivated for earlier public appearances.

Men's focus on appearance in reporting on women speakers was closely associated with the need to label and contain women—a need to maintain women's place in a hierarchy that prevented their dominance over men. Reports that focused on dress and appearance often reveal a need to maintain that place out of fear of women's power to bewitch and captivate. In his role as chair of the Connecticut Anti-Slavery Convention in May 1840, for example, Henry G. Ludlow walked out of the meeting after an assembly vote failed to sustain his refusal to permit Abby Kelley to speak. His explanation betrays his anxieties about women's power:

> I will not consent to have women lord it over men in public assemblies. It is enough for women to rule at home. It is woman's business to take care of children in the nursery. She has no business to come into this meeting, and by speaking and voting lord it over me. Where woman's enticing eloquence is heard, men are incapable of right and efficient action. . . . The magic influence of Miss Kelley's voice and beauty has carried this vote, (the vote reversing the decision of the chair). *I had enough of woman's control in the nursery. Now I am a man, I will not submit to it.* Men have not enough strength of mind to resist the magic of woman's appeal, when it is made to their gallantry. ("The Spirit of Slavery")

Ludlow's juxtaposing descriptors of magical power against those of control and domination reveal not only his fear of women but also his belief that their power comes chiefly from their feminine beauty and wiles or their complicity in some supernatural mystery. His reaction illustrates why many men worked so diligently to maintain woman's traditional place, their fear of women if not contained.

Even those reporters less critical of women speakers similarly associated women's appearance with their ability to bewitch. After its favorable description of Abby Kelley's beauty, the *Bay Street Democrat* declared,

> It was a touching piece of eloquence, and if we were ever so prone to oppress our fellows, that angel voice would at once call us back from things on earth to bow in submissiveness at the shrine of her beauty and her gentleness. No wonder that the abolitionists produce a sensation in the community, when such sweet enchantresses, with their magic wand of poetic enthusiasm, are suffered to play at will among the finest sensibilities of the soul. ("From the Bay State Democrat")

Those who admired women speakers often did so by associating them with the fragile and delicate, as opposed to the powerful and scary. Women clearly understood such fears and associations. A "Female Petitioner" to the *Hingham Gazette* noted that "whatever influence men fear, that influence they naturally endeavor to ridicule or contemn." The recent "attack on 'rights of women'" in sermons and newspaper reports, the author suggested, "leads us to infer that woman's influence is dreaded" ("Influence of Woman").

It was just such a fear that intersecting images related to women's religious and dutiful role helped to assuage, and women public figures quickly learned to make use of unconventional weapons in claiming a space more amenable to their needs. Denied many of the traditional forums and rhetorical strategies employed by men, they capitalized on the intense attention given their appearance in order to undermine criticism and to redirect audience attention to their words. While the unusual nature of women's public presentation did not rescue women speakers entirely from criticism and abuse, such women as Mott, Kelley, and the Grimkés challenged notions that breaking traditional norms was tantamount to immorality. Their play with notions of dress and appearance gave some measure of respect and safety to a space where their words could be taken seriously as they moved toward a new place for women. The pattern became one by which women would supplement their voiced rhetoric throughout the century.

2

Blooming Celebrity:
The Flowering of a National Ethos

If the dress drew the crowds that came to hear me, it was well. They
heard the message I brought them, and it has borne abundant fruit.
—Amelia Bloomer, qtd. in Thorp

*F*rances Wright met with opposition at almost every turn, but the hysterical
reaction to her appearance on the public platform and threat to religious
and social institutions allowed for the effective use of religiously associated
Quaker dress—also associated with women's authority to speak—disarm-
ing those whose arguments had centered primarily on appearance and sinful antireligion sentiments. No dress had greater impact in changing how
women speakers were perceived, however, than the reform dress: a knee-
length dress worn over loosely fitting trousers, known in the 1850s as the
Bloomer costume. This garment fixed in the national consciousness the idea
of woman as celebrity and spokesperson on political issues and established
a visual image of woman as public speaker. Criticized widely and vigorously,
women speakers nonetheless were prominently pictured in both words and
illustrations on front pages of newspapers and in popular and scholarly
periodicals, which drew large audiences to their speeches. Women, whose
dress had always associated them with particular places, now had an appearance that associated them with the platform.

Lillian O'Connor suggests that earlier women speakers had established
"that women could speak in public and remain persons of 'high moral character,'" and therefore women at midcentury concentrated on proving the
intellect. I agree that women speakers' character was less impugned by
midcentury, but O'Connor focuses on women's choice of words to establish their sense of intellectual importance. I would suggest that women

further established their credibility and right to speak publicly by proving themselves as capable writers and editors and by entering the national and international conversation—celebrities with serious contributions to contemporary discussions rather than recognized only for entertainment or kinship. Their claim to front-page exposure for serious concerns further connected them with a public place. The dress reform issue provided a topic that many women found comfort in addressing, both from the platform and in the popular press. Women continued to draw attention to their position on dress throughout the century. The dress also created great celebrity for some women, providing an authoritative ethical presence that gained viability for women as public speakers. Perhaps the most powerful rhetorical impact the new dress offered, however, was its visual presence, which associated women with a larger and more public arena.

Initially the new dress was very well accepted; however, it quickly became controversial. Nearly all criticism addressed its significance for woman's place. Some critics denounced the costume entirely, insisting that women maintain their pedestaled place in the domestic sphere. Many "moderates" who felt unable to support the dress fully because of its radical implications tried to situate its wearers according to a limited arena. Henry Ward Beecher, for example, who was "not ultra on bloomers" and admitted that "our eye is yet in bondage to the old forms," grudgingly conceded the dress's appropriateness but restricted its place: "[L]et every woman have a bloomer dress, for the sake of foot excursions" (9). A complete acceptance of the dress that represented such a radical change in woman's place would take decades; however, initial efforts to confine the new dress to specific limited places, thereby restricting a shift in ideological perspectives, failed during the dress's most sensational years.

The earliest positive rhetorical impact of the reform dress resulted from the exposure it gave women. Audiences often expected to see women speakers dressed in the costume and sometimes came expressly for that purpose. Such excitement created national celebrity for some speakers, a notoriety that drew audiences and promoted women's authority as public figures. In addition, the dress became associated with change, although that had not been its original purpose. Like other dresses assigned specific locations, such as ball gowns or garden dresses, the reform dress provided a form of attire that associated its wearer with a public arena. At the same time, dress reform was a woman's issue. Therefore, attention to this topic helped to associate radical women in public forums with a traditional concern for women and provided a public topic for women that few dared deny them.

Shaping the National Conversation

Pleas for changes in women's dress had circulated in the popular press for decades, focusing primarily on the unhealthy effects of popular clothing. Such legitimate concern, therefore, lent a measure of credibility to reforms in women's dress. Much attention had centered on the use of corsets and tight lacing to create the celebrated hourglass figure. Valerie Steele maintains that "most claims of corset-induced disease [in nineteenth-century women] are either completely invalid or greatly exaggerated" (58). But at midcentury physicians, clergy, and popular writers warned of the damage that corsetting and other aspects of conventional dress had on women's bodies, and newspapers and periodicals gave wide coverage to such concerns. Critics decried the mode of dress that "drags down everything, till not only the lungs, prevented from spreading laterally are forced to expand downwards, but all organs below the lungs are forced out of their places" ("Dress and Disease"). Physicians reported that corsets and tight lacing "sometimes put so much pressure on internal organs that the uterus was squeezed out through the vagina" (qtd. in Michie 21). In addition to corsets and tight lacing, physicians bemoaned the long skirts and trains that gathered filth from streets and allowed rain-soaked and ice-encrusted garments to gather "for the hour, about the feet and ankles" ("It Would Be More Healthy" 66). They also expressed concern about the weight (often up to fifteen pounds) of the numerous yards of fabric supported by quilted and starched petticoats that women wore to create the voluminous fashionable skirts that "embarrass the organs," and "make half our women prematurely aged, and entail on many an existence to which death would be preferable" (66). The *Presbyterian* claimed that "Fashion kills more women than toil and sorrow" ("Fashionable Women").

Concern about the ill effects of women's clothing extended beyond fear for the current generation. Health journals claimed that the restrictive clothing led to "muscular inertia" that

> render[s] our women so weekly [*sic*] as mothers, and their children so feeble that half of them die before their seventh year. As the tight-lacing of the past generation has so weakened our females that many children are dying off prematurely, so the sweepingly long skirts of the present age are paving the way for the increased disease of the future generation, as well as diminishing the number born. ("Long Skirts" 176)

Such criticisms of women's dress had become common parlance, and regardless of whether or not fashionable dress actually harmed women's bodies, reports from physicians and other leaders established widespread concern over such injury, allowing speakers to focus serious discussion around women's dress.

Some women responded by offering reform dresses intended to rectify the unhealthy effects of traditional dress. For those unable or unwilling to negotiate the delicate balance of intersecting feminine images, the costume became a pariah and effectively undermined rhetorical effectiveness. But, like Quaker women, many women speakers at midcentury successfully diverted attention from frivolous discussions of women's dress and body to ensure serious notice to concerns of women. The most successful of these, Amelia Bloomer, used dress to establish her reputation and authority as speaker. Recognizing that the reading of women's bodies played a major role in their ability to be taken seriously, Bloomer literally presented an alternative reading of those bodies. In words and pictures in her temperance and woman's rights newspaper, the *Lily,* and in her own celebrated wearing of the reform dress, Bloomer became one of the best-known women of her generation, commanding international attention for her writing and speaking in the cause of women.

Amelia Bloomer

Few women surpassed Amelia Bloomer in name recognition during her lifetime. When reporting on temperance and woman's rights meetings, even when groups included those better known to us today, such as Susan B. Anthony and Elizabeth Cady Stanton, newspapers often referred to "Mrs. Bloomer and her assistants" ("Great Gathering" 5). Bloomer's name appeared on front pages throughout the country and abroad for years, aligned with the notion of serious dress reform and other concerns of women. She never spoke in public on dress reform, and she maintained a humble demeanor in her newspaper columns, but she did, in fact, contribute to the garment's notoriety.

The Bloomer costume came to Seneca Falls, New York, in January 1851, worn by Elizabeth Smith Miller. Bloomer, Stanton, and other local women quickly added it to their own wardrobes. Bloomer also began endorsing the garment in the *Lily* in response to an editorial in the Seneca County *Courier.* Bloomer and the *Courier*'s editor had already parried on the "woman question," taking opposing sides. Therefore, when the editor commented on the unhealthy and bothersome attire normally worn by women and suggested substituting Turkish pants and a shortened dress, Bloomer reacted immediately, first expressing surprise that the *Courier* would support the reform, then endorsing the recommendation.

The *New York Tribune* picked up the conversation between the two editors and distributed it throughout the country. The national conversation on dress had begun with Amelia Bloomer at its center. Because she challenged editors' and reporters' views of the reformed dress as well as men's right to determine women's dress, she became the woman most closely associated with the new costume.

Decades of concern focusing on the injurious nature of women's dress had set the stage for women to capitalize on the conversation regarding their attire. Dress reform had been a topic for newspapers long before the *Lily* entered the dialogue, but the attention surrounding Bloomer's witty arguments, the repeated surfacing of the tunic and trousers on the nation's major streets, and significantly, the naming of the costume made the issue far more prominent. By 18 August 1851, the *New York Tribune* noted that "a paper can hardly be opened which does not have something to say about Bloomers" ("Women's Dress"). *Punch* regularly included cartoons, articles, and verses poking fun at dress reform (Blackwell 95).

The notoriety was at times uncomfortable for Amelia Bloomer, but she capitalized on the controversy. In the May 1851 issue of the *Lily*, she described the reform dress:

> Our costume is as yet by no means perfected; there is a lack of harmony in the dress we now wear, which is nothing different from the reigning fashion, except that our skirts have been robbed of about a foot of their former length, and a pair of loose trowsers of the same material as the dress, substituted. These latter *extend from the waist to the ankle,* and may be gathered into a band and buttoned around the ankle, or, what we think prettier, gathered or plaited up about two inches in depth, and left sufficiently wide for the foot to pass through, and allow for their falling over the top of the gaiter. They may be trimmed to suit the taste of the wearer. Instead of the whalebone bodice, the dress should be made with a sack front extending from the shoulder to the knee, and a tight back, with the skirt gathered in as usual; or cut the whole in the sack style—fitting the form to the waist, and then let it swell.

Two months later, she responded to readers' complaints:

> We may owe an apology to some of our readers for devoting so much of our paper to the subject of dress. We did not design saying much about it this month, but we are receiving so many communications on the subject, and there are so many of our readers who feel a deep interest in the matter, that we cannot well avoid giving it

prominence. Then too, we are standing now altogether on the defensive, and must parry, or hurl back the attacks made upon us. ("We May Owe an Apology")

The July 1851 issue contained *Lily's* first daguerreotype, featuring a woman in the "New Costume" (see fig. 2.1). Bloomer's caption read:

We take pleasure in being able to present our readers with a representation of the "New Costume." This is *not* a picture of ourself, but a correct copy of an engraving which appeared a few weeks since in the Boston "Carpet-Bag," and which was cut from a daguerreotype

Fig. 2.1. First *Lily* Bloomer daguerreotype, July 1851.

of the first lady who donned the short dress and trowsers in that city. It is the best representation we have seen of the dress. The skirt is a little shorter and the trowsers a little fuller than any we have worn; otherwise it would answer very well for us. There are a great variety of pictures in the different papers, all claiming to be "the full Bloomer costume," and all entirely unlike *us* except this one. There is nothing peculiar about the style of our dress, except that it is short, and we wear no bodice;—this we have said repeatedly, yet publishers persist in dressing us in all manner of ways, and misrepresenting us entirely. At the request of the Publishers of the BOSTON MUSEUM we stood for a daguerreotype some two or three weeks since, and that paper will contain the first and only correct likeness of us. We shall next month introduce this picture to the readers of the *Lily.*

In September 1851, Bloomer published the promised likeness of herself (see fig. 2.2). The discomfort she displays in presenting her body for such public reading is understandable given conventions applied to nineteenth-century women. Still, she obviously relishes the attention, all the while wishing the likeness were more flattering. Her caption reads:

> We are indebted to T. W. Brown of the Cayuga Chief, for the above cut, which was taken from a daguerreotype of ourself. In the main it is a very good representation of our dress, though not as perfect a one as we hoped for. The artist has failed to show the trowsers to as good advantage as we could wish. Of the face we will say nothing. Those who know us can best tell if there is any resemblance, and those who do not know us can imagine it to be a correct likeness if they choose. Our friends say it looks much older than we do. It matters but little, as we are not ambitious to show our face to our readers; all we seek is to let them see just what an "immodest" dress we are wearing, and about which people have made such an ado. We hope our lady readers will not be shocked at our "masculine" appearance, or gentlemen mistake us for one of their own sex.
>
> This picture appeared in the Chief last week accompanied by a very flattering sketch. This, modesty forbids us to copy, but if any of our readers are anxious to read it, by sending one dollar to T. W. Brown, Auburn, N.Y., they can have the privilege of doing so, and also of seeing the many good things which the Chief will be sure to contain for a year to come.

Of greater interest here is the obvious awareness of the depiction's rhetorical appeal. Bloomer believed that the likeness would undermine criticism, which she felt to be greatly exaggerated; at the same time, she hoped to sell copy and continue the highly visible alternative reading for women's bodies.

Bloomer carefully negotiated the radical change her appearance presented by balancing it with traditional images of women's place. She enhanced her appeal by appearing not to promote her own notoriety. She humbly disclaimed ownership of the reform dress, noting that Elizabeth Smith Miller was really its originator and first proponent. She referred to the dress as the

Fig. 2.2. Amelia Bloomer in Bloomer costume, *Lily*, September 1851.

"new costume" or "reformed dress," avoiding the use of her own name. Still, she repeatedly included references from other newspapers, either because they supported her position or in order to respond to those in opposition. In doing so, she furthered the connection between her name and the dress as almost all newspapers used the header "Bloomer" in order to attract attention and identify the content.

Bloomer's handling of the dress issue seems masterfully planned to heighten her celebrity. Subscriptions to the *Lily* grew rapidly. In 1851, the *Lily* had a regular monthly audience of approximately five hundred. By 1853, Bloomer was printing the newspaper semimonthly rather than monthly, and copies were selling at a rate of more than four thousand per issue. In addition, shortly after achieving national notoriety, Bloomer became a public speaker in support of the women's issues she advanced in her newspaper. As suggested by the epigraph to this chapter, she readily acknowledged that publicity surrounding the dress controversy aided in drawing large audiences wherever she spoke.

A Celebrated Ethos

Bloomer delighted in reprinting conservative editorials from other newspapers and highlighting what she considered their ridiculous nature. When the editor of the *New York Courier and Enquirer* admitted to his "unalloyed disgust" with efforts that would "break down our respect for woman" by examining "that which so nearly regards her personal sanctity," Bloomer responded in September 1851:

> The nice editor also seems to think this discussion of female costume [is] desecrating to all those gentler securities of the sex, given to us by virtue of man's respect, &c, &c. Now in the name of all that is sacred we would ask, what does woman want of all those gentler securities? ("The New Costume" 66–67)

To that editor's remark "The sun belongs to man, the shade is woman's," Bloomer responded, "What a libel is put upon the work of God in this sentence . . . as if a creature had been formed by the Divine Architect so imperfect that the shade should be suited to cover up those deformities and imperfections which the sunlight might expose" (67).

In commentaries such as these, Bloomer led the conversation on women's dress with a demonstrated rhetorical awareness of her position and constructed an ethos difficult for her opponents to attack. Always the devoted wife, Bloomer maintained her association with the home, repeatedly making references in the *Lily* to her husband, D. C. Bloomer, demonstrating her devotion and expounding upon her attention to wifely and household duties. Bloomer was childless, negating criticism that she might be neglecting her children. In addition, as demonstrated in the daguerreotype she presented, Bloomer embodied the physical traits of femininity espoused by her generation. She was petite, with small hands and feet. Public accounts pointed to her graceful and cordial bearing. Yet despite her courteous manner and "feminine" ways, Bloomer clearly understood the advantage she gained by placing herself in opposition to men in positions of authority. She appreciated the power and voice associated with the household recognition of her name.

The press gave greatest attention to the Bloomer costume during the summer of 1851. But the interest continued for years, and Bloomer herself included another representation of the modified attire in January 1852.[1] Aware of her readers' keen interest in her as a celebrity figure, even when the likenesses were not of her, she helped her audience imagine her body in the images she offered: "If our readers are curious to know which of the figures in the plate represents *our* dress most faithfully, they can imagine they see us in the sacque and bonnet" (see fig. 2.3).[2] She also took the opportunity to encourage readers to adopt the dress, all the while confirming her position as pioneer and expert:

> Although we have dearly loved our dress since its adoption, we never fully appreciated its beauties and benefits well since the coming on of winter. It is much warmer, with a smaller amount of clothing, than the old style, and there are no long skirts to gather up mud and snow, and whip it upon the ankles, or to become drabbled and frozen a foot in depth. We know that many look upon us as singular—that many frown upon us for daring to do different from the mass; but having experienced the blessings of freedom, we cannot rivet the chains upon ourself again, even to gain the good will, or to avoid the frowns of slavish conservatives. ("Our Fashion Plate")

Typically, she made this occasion an opportunity to reinforce her arguments against women's "old dress"—its dragging in the mud and snow; its unhealthy and uncomfortable binding on the upper part of the body, and wet, cold, and filthy exposure to the lower parts; and its costly, weighty, and impractical use of yards and yards of fabric. Much space in the *Lily* was given to the dress issue for the remainder of her tenure.

Bloomer's efforts at dress reform were important for public speakers because of the rupture they created in the way women's bodies were read. Conventional negative associations between women and petticoats gave way

Fig. 2.3. "Our Fashion Plate," *Lily,* January 1852.

to a new image permitting an alignment of women with public spaces and civic speaking. The costume itself, already represented in print and daguerreotype throughout the nation's newspapers, provided a public (ad)-dress. Bloomer herself became associated with civic leadership. Traditionally, a few women were illustrated in newspapers, but these were women aligned with specific acceptable roles of entertainment, for example, singers Jenny Lind and Catherine Hayes and actresses Charlotte Cushman and Fanny Kemble. Wives of famous men often attained newspaper coverage as well. Bloomer's representation was atypical, affiliating women with a public political position, and her image seemed to appear everywhere, both nationally and internationally. The daguerreotype Bloomer had made appeared in such diverse locations as the *Boston Museum* (June 1851); the *Illustrated London Times* (19 July 1851); the *New York Picayune* (July 1851); and the *Water Cure Journal* (October 1851).

Recuperating the Image of Women's Dress

If other forms of dress affiliated women with the domestic sphere, this costume created a public place for women. In addition, Bloomer deliberately challenged negative references to women's traditional dress. For example, when some newspapers began to make much of "male bloomers," that is, older men who took to wearing shawls for warmth in cold weather, she defended men's right to wear the shawl. It belonged more accurately to men, according to Bloomer, because "it answers so well to the description of the garment prescribed for them in Deuteronomy 22.12: 'Thou shalt make thee fringes upon the four quarters of thy vesture wherewith thou covered though.'" She preferred to see the shawl banished entirely because of its "requiring both hands to keep it on" thus "contract[ing] the chest and caus[ing] stooping shoulders" ("Male Bloomers" 4), and recommended sacques for both women and men because they allowed for straighter posture and free hands.

More broadly, Bloomer worked to change the negative discourse that denigrated any clothing associated with women. This rhetorical revision focused on the way articles of apparel, such as bonnets and skirts, often slipped into conversation intended to demean. No articles of women's clothing served this purpose more frequently than petticoats. The word provided derogatory commentary in literature, jokes, and conversation generally intended to humiliate men. Most notedly for the early nineteenth century, James Fenimore Cooper's characters repeatedly deride one another, questioning their masculinity with the descriptor "petticoats." Bloomer publicly protested the related practice of insulting men by offering them petticoats:

> It has long been customary for men, when they wish to express great contempt for the action of an individual, or to hold him up to the scorn and ridicule of the world, to present him with a *petticoat*. . . . The man must be degraded in the eyes of the world by the offer of a woman's garment—no other being found sufficiently expressive of the disgust of its contemners. (qtd. in D. C. Bloomer 269)

Bloomer depicted such actions as evidence of "cowardice, of meanness, of weakness, of littleness of soul." She called on women to "frown down all such acts" with regard to any part of their costume, and to stand ever ready to defend it from dishonor. According to Bloomer, "If that garment is in reality the badge of cowardice and inferiority that men would make it to be, then the sooner it is abandoned by woman and one more appropriate to her true character substituted the better." But so long as women continued to wear the garments, such ridicule that reflected on women should "receive the censures of men and the scorn of women" (269). The Bloomer costume, of course, eliminated petticoats, and Bloomer's efforts diminished the derogatory association with women's clothing.

Her notoriety gave Bloomer authority and visibility that few other women speakers could command. While her dress drew audiences, her "feminine" demeanor won respect. Repeatedly, newspapers reported their surprise that the woman who symbolized radical dress had not lost her "womanliness." A typical report is that of the *Cleveland Daily Plain Dealer:* "There is all of the lady in her every movement, in spite of the not altogether ungraceful though anomalous dress she wore" ("Mrs. Bloomer's Address" 3). And, of course, her wearing of the Bloomer seemed less questionable than for other women. Why wouldn't the woman for whom it was named wear the Bloomer?

Other Bloomer Wearers

Of all public speakers, Amelia Bloomer used the costume to best rhetorical effect, but others effectively drew audiences and praise as well. Lucy Stone, like Bloomer, "was small and slight, and one of the few women who looked well in it" (Blackwell 104). Early biographers of women speakers often focus on women's bodies when explaining their long use, or short employment, of the reform dress. Alice Stone Blackwell describes Bloomer as "small, slight, young and very pretty," suggesting that she, too, "looked well" in the costume (111), and Elizabeth Smith Miller had "a fine figure" and therefore "wore it to better advantage than any of the others" (113). Ida Harper notes that Amelia Bloomer "was pretty and little and looked well in anything she wore" (91). These women successfully defied traditional conventions for dress because their femininity in other areas softened its impact.

The reform dress was less rhetorically effective for women who were less willing or less able to negotiate intersecting images of femininity. Initially, it helped to draw audiences for all speakers who wore it. But the derogatory comments accompanying any reportage of speakers soon made the dress a liability. For example, because she broke many other strictures assigned the ideal woman, Susan B. Anthony suffered harsher criticism for wearing the dress; the Bloomer lessened rather than enhanced her rhetorical effectiveness. Harper describes Anthony as "tall, rawboned, heavy-featured" and coming "closest to the popular picture of a strong-minded woman" (91). At a time when ministers celebrated the fact that "we have redeemed women from a life of drudgery" and warned women against manual labor lest they make their "hands and feet large" (Thompson 217), calling attention to a body that came up short of expectations for women simply opened Anthony to attack. In addition, she had not married. Often describing her as an "old maid," reporters suggested that her questioning of societal norms resulted from her "disappointment" in love and her anger that no man had taken her as his wife. Anthony also lacked the soft voice and the ability to convey a relaxed and comfortable sense of parlor conversation that more accepted women speakers were able to project. To add, then, a costume that only "looked good" on dainty women simply emphasized Anthony's deviance. Wearing a dress associated with the masculine heightened other features considered to lack femininity and lessened Anthony's ethical appeal. Anthony herself acknowledged the rhetorical mistake of breaking too many societal strictures: "I learned the lesson then that to be successful a person must attempt but one reform. By urging two, both are injured, as the average mind can grasp and assimilate but one idea at a time" (qtd. in Ida Harper 117).

Opponents in the press readily seized upon such departures and focused attention on the body. Moses Beach, editor of the *New York Sun,* described Anthony's "ungainly form rigged out in bloomer costume and provoking the thoughtless to laughter and ridicule by her motions upon the platform" (qtd. in Stanton et al. 90). Later, when Antoinette Brown and Anthony spoke in Utica, New York, on behalf of temperance, *New York Courier* editor James Watson Webb noted that after concluding her speech, Anthony "gathered her short skirts about her tight pants" and sat down (qtd. in Ida Harper 83).

Other reformers, such as Paulina Wright Davis and Elizabeth Oakes Smith, chose to enhance their appeal by dressing especially fashionably in order to demonstrate that many woman's rights advocates did not transgress societal norms. Smith's earliest lectures were on such topics as "Dress, Its Social and Aesthetic Relations" (Wyman, *Two American Pioneers* 194). She claimed to be the "first woman that ever lectured before the lyceums of the country" (Wyman, *Selections* 97), and she helped to support her family through her lucrative speaking engagements. Even those who opposed her public speaking often approved her appearance because of its genteel demeanor. One especially vocal critic, Richard Grant White, nonetheless praised

> her calm, pleasant face, those soft and kindly luminous brown eyes, and that wealth of waved dark hair, drawn low over her fair white forehead, in the fashion of the time . . . the kind and tender words flowing from the faultless lips. . . . Her bearing was majestically grand, her manners refined and dignified, yet cordial, and taking her all in all, she looked, acted, and moved the born patrician. (qtd. in Wyman, *Two American Pioneers* 194)

By setting herself apart from the more notorious speakers and maintaining the appropriateness of traditional dress and appearance at the podium, Smith helped to create a public space at the rostrum for "everywoman."

Clarina Howard Nichols

The dress issue provided opportunities for numerous women to become public rhetors and furthered the visibility of those already positioned to speak publicly. Women newspaper editors often made dress reform a major topic of discussion, and many more women wrote letters and articles and had their opinions published. Clarina Howard Nichols supplemented interest in her *Wyndham County Democrat* by supporting Bloomer's efforts at dress reform. When traveling the country speaking for temperance and woman's rights, Nichols had worn matronly clothing and knitted, a characteristic commented on by newspapers wherever she traveled. She continued to gain recognition for her position and unique wit after her move to Kansas. She responded publicly to the Kansas representative who cast the only dissenting vote in an effort to give Kansas women the vote on school matters by noting, "I don't believe in this scramble for the breeches." Addressing the editor of the *Kansas Daily Commonwealth,* Nichols responded to the typical references that disparaged women by referencing dress:

> The charge has met us from the professional man to the hod-carrier, in every movement to secure to ourselves the means and the right of self government, that we were scrambling for the breeches. . . . It is evident that the bifurcated garment, by common consent of the *sovereign* people, symbolizes male supremacy or masculine authority. In view of this subject, and the antiquity and universality of the use of the term, as emblematic of male government, I suggest that the Roman-beaked bird be erased from the national escutcheon and breeches substituted. (Gambone 129–30)

On another occasion she complained, "The women of these United States are asking to be enfranchised; but there is in the way, so men tell us, *a muddy pool,* from which the foes and friends of woman suffrage are alike earnest to save our dainty skirts" (Gambone 246). Nichols's adroit way with words gave editors across the country delight in carrying her responses.

Jane Grey Swisshelm

However, the woman editor whose comments were picked up by exchanges most often after those of Amelia Bloomer was Jane Grey Cannon Swisshelm, editor of the Pittsburgh *Saturday Visiter.* Like Amelia Bloomer, Swisshelm's repartee with editors of other newspapers on the dress issue afforded her a high degree of visibility that increased her already widespread recognition. Swisshelm often used her newspaper to voice her views on proper roles with regards to women and dress. She sparred with editors and typically staked out her own territory on the matter. She mocked men who thought they had the right to determine women's dress, but she also reproved women who wore men's clothing, and she eventually refused to support the Bloomer dress categorically, often assuming an ethos of moderation.

Swisshelm had weighed in on the dress topic even before the notoriety surrounding the Bloomer costume. In an article written for the *Saturday Visiter* in June 1850, she declared, "We are at a loss to know how . . . an equality of rights between the sexes must perforce bring a similarity of attire!" She also expressed concern about the example set by Helena Marie Weber, a European proponent of masculine dress for women, and questioned the notion that "pantaloons had been the emblem of supreme authority since Adam was a little boy." The ancients, she insisted, wore flowing garments, not divided pants. Swisshelm objected to women wearing men's clothing, but she condoned the wearing of Turkish trousers for some occasions:

> There is no indelicacy, no impropriety in it; on the contrary it would be very suitable and becoming for all pedestrian exercises in the country, or in the dirty streets in California; but good taste must ever [indistinguishable] these ladies to assume the long skirt when a clean floor makes it suitable. ("Women in Male Attire" 1850)

Although Swisshelm was a staunch supporter of woman's rights, she often differed from many others who supported reform, and such opposition always gained her widespread copy in periodicals. She opposed woman's rights conventions, she said, primarily because leaders contended that there was no difference between the sexes, an idea she saw as "unnatural and preposterous." She further distanced herself from many women by using invective language. For example, in addressing those who sought "the *privilege* of wearing pantaloons," she said,

> We consider them, simply, insane. We should as lief think of contending for our *rights* to wear handcuffs, or a brass collar with somebody's name on it. Pantaloons are an emblem of servitude—were invented for the convenience of labor, and are suitable for masons, carpenters, &c., &c. ("Women in Male Attire" 1850)

In May 1851, Swisshelm was still questioning why any woman would wish to wear men's attire, still defending the Turkish Costume, "which has long been acknowledged as a most graceful and becoming feminine attire!" ("Women in Male Attire" 1851). But later in the same month, noting that "Nearly every paper we take up has something to say on the subject" and denying what some newspapers were claiming—that she herself had adopted the "new costume"—Swisshelm began to question even the wearing of Turkish trousers:

> We never thought dress of so much importance as to be worth any great act of moral heroism. We would not subject ourself to the rude gaze of a mob on the street, or the insolence of ruffians and boys, for anything less than the salvation of a soul. No dress could be comfortable or convenient to us which would gather half a dozen boys to stare at us. We should never think of being a martyr for such slight cause as the pattern of a new frock; nor have we any need to be so, for neither health nor convenience requires it. Godey, Graham, and Sartain combined could not get up a fashion that we could not, in five minutes, arrange into a comfortable, convenient, healthful costume, without making any change which would attract the attention of a casual observer. Very few will notice that a dress lacks two, three or four inches of touching the pavement when the wearer walks, yet this saves the nastiness of street sweeping. Very few will observe that a bodice, instead of being made in the form of an hour-glass, has the natural curves of the human form, and is wide enough to admit of full breathing, yet this effectually does away with all unhealthiness and inconvenience. We can walk, and climb, and dance with more ease and freedom in a whaleboned bodice than any loose sack, simply because we make the bodice to fit the waist instead of the waist to fit the bodice. Long skirts are no trouble to us, because we never have them unnecessarily heavy, and make them to rest upon the shoulders. ("Short Dresses")

Swisshelm suggested that those demanding radical reform were extremists, focusing attention on a matter of little importance. She insisted that traditional dress could easily be made safe and comfortable with a bit of common sense. Her stance and sharp comments drew attention from exchanges across the country adding to her national persona.

A Sisterly Disagreement

By July 1851, Swisshelm was using the term *Bloomer* and questioning Amelia Bloomer's position on dress, thus beginning an exchange carried not only by the *Visiter* and the *Lily* but also by newspapers throughout the country. Noting in the 26 July issue of the *Saturday Visiter* the numerous requests that she "come out in favor of the full Bloomer dress," Swisshelm stood firm. When Bloomer announced adoption of the dress, she decided, she said, because she thought so highly of Bloomer, to try the dress while working in the garden or visiting neighbors. Swisshelm related three attempts she made to wear and like the dress, partly because of its support by men and women of good taste, but primarily, she said, to oppose the "ribaldry of that gallant class of editors who think that giving laws for the length of women's petticoats is a part of their masculine prerogative." Still, expressing her own distaste for the reform dress, she told readers, "Now we give it up, convinced it is a mistake." Swisshelm enumerated all the reasons for her dislike, from the "flip flap" of loose trousers to the "falling over in a puff" of gathered ones. But her primary objection was related to her own philosophy with regards to needed reforms for women: "The whole controversy is much ado about nothing—a grand petticoat-warfare, which would appear to argue that woman never can get above dress—that in some form it must occupy the first place in her affections, the principal part of her thoughts." Although she had long been an advocate for legal reform and improved educational opportunities and suffrage for women, Swisshelm had little patience for those who disagreed with her or for those she thought created embarrassment for the cause: "It makes one blush to think of women who are great moral reformers, setting to work to fix the attention of the world upon a new-fashioned petticoat" ("The Bloomer Costume" 106).

This confrontational style contributed to Swisshelm's fame because it set her apart from both those who advocated traditional dress and those who lobbied for dress reform, and she did not hesitate to single out and castigate women dress reformers:

> We are sorry, very sorry, that Mrs. Bloomer and other women of mind, whom we had looked upon as co-laborers in the work of awaking public attention to the legal and social disadvantages under which woman labors, should have drawn off their forces to get up a doughty campaign against the bondage of petticoats. . . . If the world must needs be set by the ears about a few inches of skirt, let somebody attend to getting up the fight who is good for nothing else. ("The Bloomer Costume" 106)

For a number of years, Swisshelm responded to Bloomer's columns on dress as well as to others who wrote letters, either to the *Visiter* or *Lily* or to the *New York Tribune* or other newspapers of large circulation, and many of those responded in print. Throughout these exchanges, however, both Bloomer and Swisshelm supported a sisterhood among reform women above all. Each expressed ambivalence at disagreeing with one she held in esteem and with whom she agreed in other matters.

It is not difficult to see why the two differed on matters of dress, however. Aside from disapproving of the new costume's style, Swisshelm declared in the 20 September 1851 issue of the *Saturday Visiter,* "It is a law of God and Nature, ratified by the laws of man, that the sexes should be distinguished by dress" ("The Bloomer Dress" 138). Bloomer could never agree that woman's dress was a product of either God or Nature. But perhaps their greatest difference was in their philosophical approach about the most expedient role for gaining rights for women. Bloomer believed dress reform to be integral to overall reform for women, and she had successfully used the reform dress to draw audiences to her speeches, subscribers to her newspaper, and attention to the cause of woman's rights in general. Swisshelm's opposition put her in direct conflict with Bloomer. Swisshelm believed the attention to dress was harming efforts for woman's rights because opponents so readily used the issue to argue against all rights for women: "The most potent *argument* which has ever been brought to bear against woman's just claims to a just recompense for her labor and a voice in making the laws which govern her, has been the sneer, 'they want the pantaloons'" ("The Bloomer Costumer" 138).

Swisshelm contended that greater freedom and rights for women would "strengthen, not weaken their distinguishing traits; that it would make man more manly and woman more womanly," and she resisted any efforts that fueled the fears that

> if she were not forcibly disfranchised and legislated into the position of an inferior, she would lose all those natural peculiarities which distinguish her from man! She would become masculine—must don the pantaloons! Such is the barrier which holds woman in the position of a slave! Now this is just exactly what we have been contending against for the last eight years. It is to the overthrow of this opinion we have consecrated our life. ("The Bloomer Costume" 138)

The independent and unconventional Swisshelm found standing apart rhetorically effective. But she also had invested much of her life's work in defending those women who demanded greater rights and freedoms against charges of being "desexed" and "unfeminine." She was particularly sensitive to and concerned about any issue that added rhetorical force to her opponents' arguments. Swisshelm's attitudes may also have been influenced by past involvements. She had established a successful business as a corset maker in Louisville in 1838. Her knowledge of and appreciation for the corset industry certainly may have colored her perspectives on dress, not to mention the fact that opposing corsets unconditionally could have opened her to allegations of insincerity.

For her part, Bloomer responded formally to Swisshelm's remarks several times in the *Lily*. Commenting on Swisshelm's "faultfinding," noting her disagreement with Swisshelm as to specifics of the new dress, and drawing upon Swisshelm's own insistence that she was "sorry, very sorry," Bloomer reversed Swisshelm's criticism. As rhetorically astute as ever, Bloomer claimed to be "sorry, very sorry" that Swisshelm "'whom we had looked upon as a co-laborer in the work of awaking public attention in the legal and social disadvantages under which woman labors, should have drawn off her force to get up a doughty campaign' against the comforts of our short skirts." Bloomer thus reversed Swisshelm's criticism of her into a reprimand of Swisshelm on similar charges. Like Swisshelm, she insisted upon her own sadness at the misstep of a "co-laborer" and noted that Swisshelm had devoted "two columns of her paper for six weeks in succession to so 'silly' a subject" ("Mrs. Swisshelm").

Womanly Support

Both Bloomer and Swisshelm capitalized on their show at comradery with other women. "We hardly know what to think of Mrs. Swisshelm's course in this matter of dress," Bloomer exclaimed, pointing out the inconsistencies in Swisshelm's position and highlighting Swisshelm's use of such words as "immodest, inconvenient, uncomfortable, and suicidal" to describe the dress. But Bloomer also noted the special hurt involved in women's attack on women and refused to continue the conversation:

> We have cared nothing for all the false charges, ridicule and taunts which vulgar minds have bestowed upon us and our dress; these have been more than counterbalanced by cheering words of approval and commendation from those whose good opinions we value; but we have felt hurt at being misrepresented, belied, and censured by Mrs. Swisshelm. Yet we bear her no ill will. We have ever regarded her highly, and the strange, inconsistent, unjust course she has chosen to take will not lessen our admiration of her bold and independent spirit. We shall hold no farther [*sic*] controversy with her on this subject, and deeply regret that there has ever been occasion for us to differ. ("Mrs. Swisshelm Again")

While Swisshelm refused to support adoption of any dress radically different from conventional attire, she nonetheless challenged any male who presumed to prescribe standards for women's apparel. She openly disagreed with women dress reformers, but she quickly came to their defense when male editors presumed to criticize them. When the *Pittsburgh Commercial*

Journal accused those who wore the Bloomer of being "itchers for notoriety," calling the dress a substitute for the dress of modest women, and, according to Swisshelm, "attempt[ed] to show that those women who have appeared in this dress in Philadelphia are persons of ill fame," Swisshelm expressed shock at the editor, her "friend" and "gentleman" Mr. Riddle, for his "rudeness to a woman." Noting her own distaste for the attire, she took exception to the *Journal's* "contradistinction" between "the apparel of a modest woman" and the "modest women [who] wear it" ("The Journal and Bloomer Dress"). Swisshelm claimed,

> We have a pretty intimate acquaintance with the private character of quite a number of the ladies who are leaders in this new fashion, and know that their reputation for modesty and moral worth is above rational impeachment. They stand in these respects above the common level, and all the mistakes they can make about the pattern of a dress can never invalidate their claim to stand in the foremost ranks of the good and pure of their sex. We hate the dress most thoroughly, but respect the women who introduce it and are laboring for its adoption. ("The Journal and Bloomer Dress")

Swisshelm's adherence to traditional conventions for women with regards to appearance enabled her to more forcefully reprimand those editors who appeared "ungentlemanly" and to confront them when their representations of other women were untruthful. She assumed the persona of a rational, moderate woman negotiating and making sense of the two extremes represented by women dress reformers on the one hand and ostentatious conservative men on the other. Later, when Riddle disclaimed any intention of casting aspersions on the reputation of those wearing the new dress, but on the dress only, Swisshelm insisted that his language could only be interpreted in the way she had done so but agreed not to quarrel with him: "We care not how roughly he handles the dress, so he is just to the wearer" ("The Journal and Bloomer Dress").

Similarly, when the editor of the *Pittsburgh Post* repeatedly criticized Amelia Bloomer for her position on women's dress, Swisshelm accused him of having "Bloomer-tremens" and wondered at his great concern about her "friend Amelia," noting that if Bloomer were a widow she would "suspect her of jilting the poor fellow" ("The Post and the Bloomers"). So, much as family members do, Swisshelm felt perfectly comfortable taking to task sisters with whom she disagreed, but she had no patience for men who felt it their prerogative to criticize them.

Attention to dress helped to further a celebrity reputation for both

Bloomer and Swisshelm. Their witty styles, deliberate criticisms of one another, and mocking attention to reproaches from men captured the imagination of newspaper editors and readers across the country. They conversed nationally with male editors of newspapers with large circulation, becoming major participants in conversations on front pages that had earlier excluded women from such coverage. Their national (and for Bloomer international) celebrity created an authority and accompanying credibility that contributed to acceptably enlarged spaces which women would continue to expand. They successfully appropriated the subject of women's dress for women and helped to reconstruct women's body image from a negative one associated only with petticoats to one of greater purpose and fluidity, the public quality of the new dress helping to create a more visible and acceptable place for women rhetors.

The *Sibyl* Continues Reform

The height of the sensation over the Bloomer and dress reform lasted barely four years. By 1855, many of the original and most notorious proponents of the reform dress had abandoned it. Still, a considerable number persevered. Amelia Bloomer sold the *Lily* in 1855 when she moved to Iowa, and the newspaper ceased publication in 1856. But Lydia Sayer Hasbrouck's *Sibyl* assumed leadership on dress reform. From July 1856 to June 1864, the *Sibyl* published women's letters and stories and sparred with such highly visible opponents as Genio Scott, fashion editor for the *Home Journal.* The *Sibyl* also faithfully published proceedings and speeches from the National Dress Reform Association. Ironically, Hasbrouck increased circulation for her newspaper by "clubbing" it with popular fashion periodicals. That is, she arranged to have the *Sibyl* offered, along with such popular magazines as *Godey's* and *Peterson's,* at reduced prices. For example, when Ann Stephens began her *New Monthly Magazine,* the annual subscription cost was $1.50, but a subscriber could receive both the *New Monthly Magazine* and the *Sibyl* for $2.00 ("Book and Magazine Notices" 11). For more popular periodicals, such as *Godey's,* a subscriber could often receive both at the price of the more established magazine.

When criticized for such promotions, Hasbrouck responded, "Magazines contain much that is good" and "It is not right to divest life of all its charms of beauty, especially to the young, and *Godey's* and *Peterson's,* &c., are full of useful cuts and hints toward this, which we cannot give in the *Sibyl.*" In addition, the periodicals offered "excellent thoughts" and helpful instructions in drawing, household hints, and other valuable assistance. Finally, and probably most important for Hasbrouck,

There are some conservatives who would not take the *Sibyl* were it not they got both papers for the price of one singly; they read, reflect, compare, and the results are often good. These magazines offer to club with us, people know the nature of them, and need not take them if they do not wish them. For our part, we wish to see them; to get them we must give them some notice or advertisement, (our paper being worth much less than theirs,) or else pay their subscription price, which we can't afford just now. We fail to see that we do wrong in doing this, and must say that *Peterson's, Godey's,* and other magazines contain much of interest to us, aside from their ridiculous Fashion Plates. ("The Fashion Magazines" 276)

Women continued their work for dress reform in other ways, gaining adherents for their position and increasing acceptance of women's public presence. A younger generation of speakers and writers joined the elders, adding their own uniqueness. Probably most notable was Elizabeth Stuart Phelps, a noted author who wrote and gave lectures on dress reform in the latter part of the century.

Jane Grey Swisshelm continued to realign her position and garner national attention. After terminating her own newspaper, Swisshelm wrote for such popular periodicals as the *Independent,* insisting on the need for dress reform and, as always, defending women and placing much blame on men. When the passenger liner *Atlantic* sank and women might have been saved had they not been wearing voluminous skirts, Swisshelm wrote,

What would men on the "Atlantic" have said had they come on board in dresses in which they could have climbed a mast, in case of shipwreck, or which would have afforded them warmth and protection without dragging them down, when submerged. . . . Men must help woman up the ladder, as they have helped her down, or they never can reach a place of common sense on which such follies would be impossible. ("The Follies of Woman's Dress" 924)

Women often capitalized on such tragedies to accent the need for dress reform. Phelps also highlighted the sinking of the *Atlantic* to insist on dress reform, narrating such comments of those who tried to rescue passengers from the sinking ship as those that follow:

Every effort was made to assist the women up the masts and out of danger till help arrived, but *they could not climb,* and we were forced to leave them to their fate. . . . When the survivors of the "Atlantic" filed past, "Not a woman among them! My God! . . . When I consider these things, I feel that I have ceased to deal with *blunders* of dress and have entered the category of *crimes*." (21-22)

The *Sibyl* highlighted such problems as well, making much of accidental burnings when women's skirts ignited from the open flames prevalent throughout nineteenth-century households and places for social gatherings and entertainments. The newspaper recognized especially such high profile cases as the death by fire of the marchioness of Salisbury and two sisters of the British nobility, Ladies Charlotte and Lucy Bridgeman. While acknowledging such widely publicized accidents, the newspaper used them to advantage to accent other accidents involving dress. For example, the newspaper often warned of "danger from fire, or wind, or water, or carriage-wheels, or rails, or pails, or in short, everything [women] encounter" ("Dress and the Victims" 662). The *Sibyl* also reported accidents where dress created problems for lesser known women, such as that of the London woman who tripped on her skirts as she ran to catch the train at London Bridge Station: "The handle [of her parasol] passed through her heart, and perforated her right lung. Cause—she wore a long dress. Had it been shorter, she would not have fallen" ("A Woman Recently" 340).

The Bloomer dress itself, along with other variations of the reform dress, continued in use throughout the century, although less prominently in most cases. Sporadic reports noted the appearance of the costume on the nation's streets, but more commonly the dress was used at rest cures and for exercise. As had Henry Ward Beecher earlier, many who had not supported widespread use of the dress attempted later in the century to assign a specific place for the costume. By January 1858, *Godey's,* which had refused to give space or credence to the Bloomer during the time of its greatest popularity, was recommending the dress for gymnastic exercise (see fig. 2.4). The feature described "the Metropolitan Gymnastic Costume" as having "a basque waist, full skirt, and Turkish sleeves and pants. The material may be either fine flannel, or French merino, of any two colors that will contrast prettily." *Godey's* assured readers, "This unique and charming costume is exceedingly comfortable and appropriate *for the purpose for which it is designed*" (emphasis mine).[3]

The bicycle finally brought the Bloomer, or a variation of it, into more general usage. Periodicals regularly presented forms of the Bloomer as appropriate for riding bicycles, and even such women as Frances E. Willard, popular president of the Woman's Christian Temperance Union, wore or promoted the divided skirt for such exercise.[4]

Despite the delayed success of the reform dress, the Bloomer served a rhetorical purpose for women speakers and writers. It drew attention to and promoted credibility for women as public figures. At the same time, the controversy highlighted the gendered nature of dress, making visible the constructed nature of women's femininity/gender. Most important, the dress contributed to an image that associated women with the public sphere.

Fig. 2.4. The Metropolitan gymnastic costume, *Godey's Lady's Book,* January 1858.

3

Restraining Women's Rhetoric:
Backlash Against the Reform Dress

I see Woman rise from her Petticoats, as *the long-imprisoned But-*
terfly rises from its crippling and *confining sheath.* That Butterfly in
its *Caterpillar condition* crawled upon the Earth, and *licked up the*
Mud and the Dirt, and now behold it, *opening and shutting* its Beautiful Wings *in the Air;* now balancing upon *a Carnation,* and now
upon *a Rose.* That Butterfly, my Sisters—(*I will, I must* be bold
enough to say as much)—that Butterfly is *a Bloomer!*
　　　　　　—"Mrs. Bloomer to the Female Race," *Punch*

*I*n May 1851, amid national excitement about dress reform, Clarina Howard
Nichols informed readers of her *Wyndham County Democrat,* "The gentlemen editors are, with one or two exceptions, exceedingly taken with the
Turkish costume which seems to have appeared nearly simultaneously in
the principal inland cities and villages of the Eastern and Western states"
("The New Fashion for Ladies' Dress"). Nichols accurately represented press
reaction to the new dress. The Bloomer initially enjoyed great support and
popularity, as newspaper editors across the country commented on the dress
when it appeared in their locality. The *New Haven Journal,* in noting "the
general admiration for those wearing the costume on the city's street," assured Connecticut readers that "those who were fortunate enough to see
the costume think it decidedly pretty" ("The New Female Costume" 3 June
1851). The *Cleveland Herald* praised the new dress, thankful for its replacement of the "spine destroying dress" ("The New Female Costume" 27 May
1851). In Kenosha, Wisconsin, the *Telegraph* "admire[d] the independence
of the ladies who dare do as they please" because they were "tired of using
their dresses to sweep the crossings and side walks" ("The New Costume—
How it Takes to the Rural Districts"). A Kentucky editor found the new

dress "femininely graceful, convenient, tidy, and in harmony with the laws of health" ("Favorable Notices of the Press"). As newspapers across the country reported the vogue of the new dress, nearly all commented on its appropriate and attractive appeal, even claiming that the women who wore the dress looked "more like angels than ever" ("We Predict") and proclaimed that it would "spread like wild-fire" ("Change in Female Costume"). Newspapers from such disparate regions as Green Bay, Wisconsin, and Detroit in the Midwest, to Portland, Maine, and Boston in the East, Atlanta and Apalachicola, Florida, in the South, and San Francisco in the Far West reported the appearances of the new dress on their streets almost universally with praise (Gattey 62–63; "Bloomer Costume Improved"; "The New Costume for Ladies" 12 June 1851; "Bloomers in California").

Even those who had not seen the costume joined the conversation by proffering opinions as to its merits. Exchanges regularly included columns listing favorable comments about the new style from newspapers across the country, ensuring that readers everywhere became informed about the proliferation of the costume and its advantages over traditional women's dress. Editors in areas where the dress had not appeared hoped "it will not be long till the ladies of our land—our own peerless beauties of Madison [Iowa]—will shed and shorten their surplus skirts" ("Bloomer's Turkish Trowsers"), and a writer in Washington, D.C., looked "forward with pleasure to the day in which every well-dressed lady will be attired in garments as graceful and becoming as are the 'frock and pants' we see described in the northern papers" ("The New Costume for Ladies" 27 May 1851). Still others would "welcome its advent as a happy release of our wives, daughters and sweethearts from the self-imposed task of sweeping the dust or mud off street crossings" ("The Ladies' New Dresses").

Editors took pride in the innovative and timely acceptance of the dress by women of their city. When the *Rochester Daily Times* announced secret caucuses in May 1851 by local women to consider adopting the dress, the *Syracuse Journal* proudly asserted, "Our Ladies have not waited for anything of this kind. It is now no uncommon thing to meet, in passing through our streets, several ladies in the new costume" ("The Turkish Costume"). Women were encouraged to follow the example of their sisters in "cast[ing] off the street sweepers" with the assurance that "their gentlemen friends, old and young, will bear them out in it, and admire them the more, and love them the better" ("Short Dresses in Milwaukee").

Bloomer activities flourished. Women held Bloomer balls and parties throughout Ohio ("Bloomer Ball"; Gattey 62) and in Greenfield, Massachusetts ("The New Female Costume" 24 June 1851). In New York City, a floral festival included speeches on dress and health with a procession of women dressed in Bloomers ("A Bloomer Festival"). A similar festival was held in Springfield, Massachusetts ("Bloomerism" 15 November 1851). Other cities boasting of Bloomer processions included New York, Battle Creek, Toledo, and Cleveland (Gattey 62). New York and Philadelphia held Bloomer concerts with appropriate musical numbers, some written specifically to honor the costume ("Bloomer Promenade"; "Bloomerism" 28 Au-

Fig. 3.1. Sheet music for "Bloomer Waltz." Courtesy of the Library of Congress.

gust 1851; "The Bloomer Schottisch"). In Lowell, Massachusetts, mill operatives wearing the Bloomer held a Fourth of July procession and subsequently organized a Bloomer Institute for promoting education and dress reform ("Bloomerism in the Mills"; Gattey 62). Musical scores and plays honored the dress (see figs. 3.1 and 3.2; see also Gattey, illustrations between pages 64 and 65). One of the more interesting Bloomer phenomenon appeared in the windows of Bunnell and Price, New York booksellers and stationers: a life-sized wax figure dressed in Bloomer costume ("Bunnell and

Fig. 3.2. Sheet music for "The New Costume Polka." Courtesy of the Library of Congress.

Price"); another, a ship whose chosen figurehead was "a full-length carved image of a female in the new Turkish Costume" ("The Bloomer Costume" 2 July 1851: 2). Others capitalized on the situation to bring attention to their activities. In St. Louis, large crowds gathered to see a young woman "walk a mile an hour for five hundred consecutive hours—graceful and rapid walker—dressed in full Bloomer costume" consisting of "a pink dress, pink trousers, and bonnet trimmed with cherry colored ribbon" ("A Female Pedestrian" 6). Pride that American women would no longer be subservient to Paris fashions added strength to the movement.

As noted by numerous editors, the success of the Bloomer was beginning to appear inevitable. In noting that the Bloomer was "graceful, convenient, tidy, and in harmony with the laws of health," for example, the *Syracuse Standard* claimed, "The dress has become too common here to attract attention, and all agree to its neatness, and the improved appearance of the wearer." The *Albany Knickerbocker* insisted that the "Turkish trowsers will eventually come in vogue" (6), and the Geneva *Gazette* predicted "a speedy and general introduction of an improvement so desirable" and declined to "enumerate the advantages attending such an improvement in personal attire" because they were so obvious ("The New Costume—How It Takes in the Rural Districts").

As women began to appropriate the conversation about their own dress, men provided support; however, as the conversation grew, and as the Bloomer gained adherents, journalists began to recast the positive rhetoric, inaugurating a backlash in the press. As discussed in chapter 5, the radical shift in the press's treatment of the reform dress motivated women speakers to alter their own rhetorical use of dress.

Such a reaction on the part of the media is perhaps understandable, since editors and publishers considered fashion their domain. Daily newspapers often relied on fashion columns, reporting "original coiffures" or "the many pretty toilettes" appearing at "fashionable soirées," as well as intermittent accounts from Paris describing the latest in fashion there ("Fashions for February"). The fashion magazines, of course, provided literature, crafts, and various features of interest to women, but the most popular, such as *Godey's* and *Sartain's,* promoted their publications largely based on Parisian fashion plates, boasting of the cost and uniqueness of such plates. Even fashion periodicals, however, had regularly called for reform in women's dress. Obviously many factors contributed to the reaction to the dress; however, as the Bloomer became associated with independent women and a changed station for them, even journalists who had espoused reform decided they would not have dress reform at the expense of changing women's role.

A Second Thought

As the reform dress gained international popularity, newspapers and periodicals that relied on fashion interests and dictated norms for women's dress lashed out against the drastically changed apparel for women. Men had been the chief prescribers of women's dress. Even those who had supported greater rights and equality for women found themselves unable to accept radical change in dress, the sign that so markedly delineated "femininity" and the separation of the sexes. Regardless of the Bloomer costume's specific purpose as outlined in chapter 2, controversy and opposition focused primarily on the new dress's pantaloons, symbol of men's authority and women's changing ideas about freedom and place. In a move equal in rhetorical sophistication to that of the dress's promoters, journalists reformulated early rhetoric in support of the dress. Ignoring wearers' claims that the costume addressed issues of comfort and health, they orchestrated an attack that impugned wearers' modesty and morality, implied a physical danger to patrons of the dress, and finally heaped ridicule on them.

New York Tribune

Early arguments of immodesty and immorality came largely from eastern newspapers. The *New York Daily Tribune,* the most widely distributed newspaper in the country at the time, had first called positive attention to the Bloomer in April 1851. While not offering explicit support, the *Tribune* suggested as much in its daily printing of praise for the costume from newspapers across the country. Within two months, half of the newspaper's columns not devoted to advertising held favorable comments on the dress garnered from exchanges. However, by mid-June 1851, the *Tribune* responded with derision to the much publicized remarks of the architect of the Crystal Palace, the enormous hall built for the 1851 World's Fair in London. Joseph Paxton had elicited a great deal of merriment by relating his unnecessary inconvenience and expense in designing a machine to clean the floors of the Palace. According to Paxton, he never used the machines because "the building had been kept completely clean by the rich silk dresses of the ladies" ("The Revolution in Dress"), a point many in the reform movement used to underscore the need for changed attire.

Commenting on Paxton's remarks as though dichotomous standards for women and men were both natural and unchangeable, the *Tribune* insisted that "Beau Nasty" was one thing but "Belle Nasty" was entirely different. Playing on the immaculate and pure image expected of "fair matrons and maidens," the editorial jested at the "filth of fifty thousand pair of boots daily gathered in from all the lanes and streets of London, only to be transferred to the rich silk dresses, and thence, in great measure, no doubt, to the rich silk hose of London's fairest matrons and maidens." After exposing difficulties with current fashions, however, rather than championing the reform dress as one might expect, the *Tribune* instead questioned the purity and decency of those who wore the Bloomer costume. The lengthy editorial offered arguments against the reform dress that would be enlisted by subsequent critics. According to the editor, nature clothes all her children "with scrupulous care"; but for man, who must clothe himself, that attire is symbolic and a matter of decency. For the *Tribune,* immodesty was obviously much more closely related to women's appropriation of masculine clothing and overstepping their place than to bodily exposure; response came in the form of a thinly veiled threat. Claiming that the costume would "unhinge our reverence for the best of mothers and stifle our affection . . . for the most amiable wives," the editor called the wearer of the costume a "heathenish caricature of masculinity" ("The Revolution in Dress").

The accusations of immodesty were both political and narrow. Because of strict nineteenth-century conventions regarding women's purity, no charges more readily threatened nineteenth-century women than those of immorality and immodesty. Claims that the new dress was indecent would have made many women fearful of adopting the dress. But the charges also exemplify men's yoking of modesty with women's confining traditional role. Although the reform dress was far more modest in coverage than traditional dress, its assumption of characteristics traditionally associated with men and with places from which women were restricted evoked charges of indelicacy and shame.

New York Herald

Immediately after the attack by the *Tribune,* the *New York Herald,* another newspaper that had printed praise from exchanges across the nation, moved coverage of dress reform to its front page and assailed the morality of wearers of the dress even more directly:

> Notwithstanding the unqualified approval given by a portion of the press for the universal adoption of the Turkish costume by the young women of America, it is an incontrovertible fact that those who have hitherto exhibited themselves in our fashionable thoroughfares decked in the new style of dress are females of very questionable character. ("The New Female Dress")

Proclaiming the dress "dangerous to good morals and subversive of virtuous sentiment in the minds of both males and females," the *Herald* chose to ignore the dress itself and, as was typical of opponents to changes for women throughout the century, assailed the characters of women who dared seek reform. Disregarding deeper implications of women's need for protection—that it was primarily from men that they needed protection—the newspaper declared,

> No virtuous female who appreciated that retiring modesty and unassuming grace which can alone adorn her sex and elevate her in the eyes of the moral and good would venture out, unaccompanied and unprotected in the most densely crowded thoroughfares of New York, bedecked in a garb which renders her the conspicuous object of rude and obscene comment by the licentious and vulgar. (1)

The *Herald* thus evoked women's supposed responsibility for men's morality and related it to the new costume: When men behaved badly, women's dress provoked such behavior. By attacking the wearers of the reform dress even more brazenly than the *Tribune,* the *Herald* placed itself in competition with the *Tribune* for the most sensational and vicious attacks on the Bloomer.

Naming the Reform Dress

Not to be outdone by the *Herald,* the *Tribune* escalated its attack on the reform dress and its wearers and helped to ensure the costume's name. Readers had offered names for the dress, most commonly the "American" dress. Those suggesting this name pointed with pride to its symbolic rejection of European fashion domination in favor of unique styles appropriate for American women. Other names surfaced as well, most often that of Camilla, in honor of the Latin virgin who wore her dresses shortened so as to participate in activities in the spirit of her patron, Diana. Either the "American" name or that of the classic Camilla as the permanent label for the dress might have prompted continued favorable attitudes toward the dress. However, this did not happen.

Picking up the term *bloomerism,* which had been used sporadically by the Massachusetts exchanges, the *Tribune* launched its most severe attack on the costume and firmly established the dress's name. The newspaper offered an image of wearers as blossoming and showy, intent on pilfering men's breeches with all the symbolic and actual authority associated with them. According to the *Tribune,*

> It is useless to cling to the skirts of the matter any longer. Our fair friends will *Bloomerize* themselves. They will tram just as they please—will have it their own way, whether that way be long or short.

They propose to inaugurate Flora as their patron saint and to carry the world under a mask of flowers." ("Bloomerism" 1 July 1851)

The notion of display became associated with the dress that had been designed and promoted specifically for its practicality, modesty, and simplicity. Both women and men regularly used flower terminology symbolically in the nineteenth century, and periodicals often ran descriptions of flowers with their representative meanings. But the delight in attaching the name "Bloomer" to the dress obviously derives from the suggestions of immodest "blooming"—or the exposing of previously covert assets—on the part of the wearers of the new dress.

Warnings to Women

Choosing to "warn all recalcitrant pantaloons betimes," the *Tribune* quoted a source "wiser than we." Because of its implied physical threat to Bloomer wearers, that warning is worth quoting at length:

> "I have always said it: Unbeaten Woman lords it o'er the world! . . . We males swagger, and talk of our superiority, but only the Savage has practical dominion over the "weaker sex," simply because he bangs his recalcitrant female in lordly style! We don't beat our women, and are therefore slaves: we are forced to knock under because we have fastidious scruples about knocking them down! This may be quite correct. I only state the fact, without commentary. Unbeaten Woman is a Tyrant. The weaker they are the more tyrannical. A little blonde creature with fair eyes and fragile figure, whom you could crush in your manly grasp, somehow or other you find yourself trembling before, as before a crowned potentate. She bends you to her purposes, to her caprices; if you resist, her pretty eyes flash scornful fire; if you quail not before her anger, she rushes into hysterics! What is helpless—and, above all, *clubless* man to do! Be meek and acquiescent!" ("Bloomerism" 1 July 1851)

Changes in dress thus brought forth a mournful complaint about eroding male superiority based on restricted force and evoked fear of further wearing away such power. If aspersions to women's modesty and morality were inadequate to derail the popularity of the dress, direct threats might be more effective. Regardless of an emphasis on the civility and modesty of women, the editorial continued to lament a loss brought on by civilization, citing men's literary tradition of angst about women and society that stressed romantic notions concerning men's authority and freedom:

That I take to be one of the primordial laws of civilization. Directly man emerges from the savage state, he becomes woman's prey. I find it the eternal theme of literature. In one shape or another it is always Samson laying his shaggy head in the fair lap of Dalilah. From Homer to Paul de Kock the story of Cyrnon and Iphigenia, which Mr. Dryden told in resounding couplets—has been varied in its incidents, but has preserved its kernel of sentiment, which is none other than the dominion of Beauty.—The old lion who allowed the fair maiden to draw his teeth and clip his terrible claws, what is that but the symbol of our daily folly? Do we not all stoop from our pedestal and crouch beneath the merciless grace of women? ("Bloomerism" 1 July 1851)

In many ways the *Tribune*'s response is surprising even apart from the obvious threat. Horace Greeley, editor of the *Tribune,* generally championed women's reform issues. He was one of the few editors to support the early woman's rights conventions, including the 1848 meeting at Seneca Falls. Later he would attend and report favorably upon women's temperance and woman's rights activities. On the other hand, as for many men, and indeed for many nineteenth-century people in general, Greeley found reform comfortable only to a point. His own prejudices and pet concerns often bisected those of other reformers. For example, in spite of his strong support of both temperance and equal rights for women, when reformers began to insist upon women's right to divorce when married to abusive drunkards, Greeley dissented, publishing lengthy tirades against divorce on any grounds except adultery. Perhaps, then, we should not be surprised that a man who was unable to relinquish his ideas on the sanctity of marriage and woman's subservience to it, even when she found herself in an abusive situation, would be unable to accept radical change in women's dress, the essence of difference between the sexes for those of his generation. His opposition was not atypical of reformers. Earlier, Theodore Weld, John Greenleaf Whittier, and other men among the abolitionists had insisted that the Grimké sisters should ignore issues of woman's rights lest they harm the cause of the slave. Greeley and later reformers, including Henry Blackwell, beseeched women reformers to discard the reform dress lest it harm other reforms—abolition, temperance, and woman's rights.[1]

Threats of bodily harm continued as the newspaper reported dangers to wearers without substantiation. One such report claimed that crowds gathering in the Bowery to ogle Bloomer wearers "increased in numbers and decreased in gallantry, until near Houston-st. the police were obliged to interfere and remove two of the critics to prison" while the Bloomers sought refuge inside a shop ("City Items"). When an observer of the Bloomers in the Bowery protested that the crowd report was untrue and that the Bloomer wearer had merely entered a saloon for refreshment, not a milliner shop for escape, the *Tribune*'s response was that there was "more than one abbreviated skirt in the City, and our informant undoubtedly had reference to another person" ("The Short-Skirt Affair in the Bowery"). Despite its claim that "Bloomers are getting to be too general to excite surprise or ridicule" ("Bloomers" 19 September 1851), the *Tribune* continued such tactics by noting the "hooting, halloing" and large crowds surrounding wearers of the dress and claimed, "Police deemed it advisable to interfere, and the bloomers were apprehended by Officer Cochran and locked up in the Fifth Ward Station House" ("Bloomers" 1 October 1851). The report of imprisonment for Bloomer wearers is highly questionable, but the *Tribune*'s account carried a message of physical threat that would surely have detracted from the Bloomer's appeal.

Political threats complemented threats to the body. *The Ladies' Wreath* carried an eight-and-a-half-page article entitled "The Bloomer Dress," in which Professor William Nevin claimed to be "seriously alarmed at this untoward display of the trowsers" with its intent of demolishing "all distinctive grades and orders" (253). Nevin attached the Bloomer to "Fourierism or Socialism, or fanaticism" (254) and believed the trowsers "one of the many manifestations of that wild spirit of socialism or agrarian radicalism" so "*rife* in our land" (253). The new dress, therefore, posed a danger to the political well-being of the entire nation: "Just in proportion as these levellers may succeed in destroying the national distinctions of character and sex between us, in the same proportion also undoubtedly will they succeed in destroying all moral government and civilization" (253). Bloomer wearers had become unpatriotic.

Members of the clergy also saw a threat to morality and modesty. In Easthampton, Massachusetts, Pastor Stone threatened to excommunicate two young women for wearing the "immodest" Bloomer, and additional reports surfaced of ministers who used the Sunday podium to protest against the indecent dress ("Short Dresses"). It seemed that every man in a position of authority was an expert on women's clothing.

Criticism and threats turned to ridicule. In August 1852, the *Cleveland Daily Plain Dealer* repeated a report from the Rochester *American* as follows:

> I saw on Broadway to-day an application of the Bloomer costume which pleased me and it was not offensive to my notions of modesty. The trousers were of blue nankeen, with flowing instead of gathered

bottoms, just making a bewitching exposure of the feet and ankles for a beautiful *dray horse*. . . . The flies and the blacksmith are the only opponents of this style. ("A New Bloomer")

Some opponents found fun in ridiculing Bloomers and African Americans at the same time, by making a present of "the Turkish costume and a gypsy hat" to a "colored lady" in Syracuse. Amelia Bloomer responded by noting the uncustomary act of showing "so much regard to the wants of colored women" and expressed the hope that the act would "make the lady truly grateful for the gift" and that "the young men [would] be equally liberal to others" ("A Colored Lady"). Most often, newspapers mixed signifiers for gender. When reporting on women's temperance and woman's rights conventions, newspapers routinely referenced "notabilities in breeches and in petticoats" or "women in trousers," even when no women wore pants or pantaloons ("Women's Rights and Duties").

Cartoonists effected much humor at the expense of Bloomers as well. Usually coupling the Bloomer dress with other efforts at change for women, lampoons graced newspapers and periodicals both nationally and internationally. The *Lantern* presented a "dissipated Bloomer" aggressively pursuing physical intimacy with a reluctant lover, and *Harper's* toyed with problems that "Lady Doctresses" might expect to encounter: Both assertive women appeared in full Bloomer costume. Because of its popularity and because many newspapers and periodicals reprinted its comments and cartoons, *Punch* influenced attitudes toward the dress. During the second half of 1851, for example, Bloomer jests appeared more than thirty times in *Punch*. The magazine lampooned leaders of the dress reform movement with fictionized letters, printed humorous verses about the costume modeled on well-known Tennyson poems, presented spoofs on "ladies' meetings," with leaders dressed in the Bloomer (see fig. 3.3), and published elaborate caricatures.[2] The periodical even devoted a double-paged spread to depictions of Bloomers (see fig. 3.4).

Fashion Magazines' Quiet Scorn

The very popular fashion magazines undermined support for the Bloomer outfit more quietly. During the early months of the sensation, they simply ignored it. When they finally confronted the controversy, they did so with barely disguised disgust or with feeble support. Most avoided direct attack on the costume, sometimes using silence as a weapon. Louis Godey acknowledged, "Our very silence, however, might have assured our readers, as well as our contemporaries of the press, that we did not look upon the proposed innovation with the least approval or favor" (189). Because the magazines professed their authority as arbiters of dress and fashion, their neglect of the subject was in itself important. Those who did acknowledge the dress often did so with scorn or half-hearted attempts to show interest.

Godey's Lady's Book

The most famous of the fashion magazines, *Godey's,* chose to ignore the national obsession with the Bloomer costume that played out throughout the summer of 1851.[3] Bloomer had begun her defense of the dress in January, and the *Lily* and several other newspapers had offered a daguerreotype of the costume by early summer. Although editors at *Godey's* were necessarily aware of the commotion surrounding the Bloomer dress, and in spite of the fact that the editor complained as late as the August issue of the "'painful dearth of incident' . . . in the world of fashion," *Godey's* chose to ignore the reform costume ("Chit-Chat of the August Fashions" 128).

Godey's finally commented in the September 1851 issue, not under the fashion columns but as a direct explanation in the "Publisher's Department." Both the placement of the explanation and the wording suggest that the editor, Sarah Josepha Hale, did not participate in the decision. Acknowledging repeated requests from readers that *Godey's* take a position on the

Fig. 3.3. "Woman's Emancipation," *Punch,* 1851.

new dress, the publisher, Louis Godey, professed faith that "as in regard to all other questions relating to their own dignity, propriety, and convenience, the ladies would eventually settle [the question] satisfactorily for themselves." Having claimed for women the right to choose the style of dress for themselves, however, Godey quickly questioned the rationale of the new dress by noting that "we have never been the advocates of hasty or unconsidered changes" ("The New or Proposed New Costume").

Such comments, of course, reflected negatively on the feasibility of the new dress. *Godey's,* a periodical based largely on the fashion industry, had for many years discussed the importance of dress and the need for reform. Despite insisting that *Godey's* need not define the numerous obvious reasons why the new dress would fail, the publisher immediately provided that reasoning:

> It is this: that the very differences which exist in the peculiar points and in the shape and structure of the human form, will be the single obstacle that will tend more than all the rest to prevent the adoption of this new style of dress. ("The New or Proposed New Costume")

Suggesting that traditional dress was the only form appropriate for women's figures, the writer called, as had the *Tribune,* for a shortening of traditional dresses as the only necessary reform. Although *Godey's* continued to make occasional protests against women's long dresses and trains, it made no

Fig. 3.4. "Bloomeriana: A Dream," *Punch,* 1851.

further comment on the Bloomer or on other facets of dress reform. The refusal to see women's bodies in any terms other than those represented by the confining and frivolous costumes of the period exemplifies the need to keep all images of women's and men's bodies clearly separate in representation and in function.[4]

Two of the Philadelphia fashion magazines, *Sartain's* and *Peterson's,* actually carried "fashion plates" of the Bloomer costume.[5] Although *Sartain's* failed to acknowledge the uproar over the Bloomer throughout most of 1851, it finally conceded the dress's news value in the September issue. Having come late to the Bloomer controversy, the magazine would not be outdone. It carried not one but three illustrations of the Bloomer costume, two for adult women and one for children (see fig. 3.5).

Sartain's, a magazine that prided itself on being "American" and delivering to readers a product made up wholly of literature by American writers, declined to take a position either favoring or opposing the dress. Instead, it chose to "refer to it merely as an item of news and matter of fact." The comment does, however, praise the "Americaness" of the dress: "We are pleased to see an attempt made by American ladies to break the thraldom in which they have been so long held, in matters of fashion, by the *artistes* of Paris and London." *Sartain's* credits American women with as much "good sense and good taste" as those from other countries and therefore with

Fig. 3.5. Adult and child Bloomers, *Sartain's,* September 1851.

a right to their own fashions. Providing minimal description because "they speak for themselves," *Sartain's* never mentioned the Bloomer again. The continued emphasis on European fashion in the most "American" of women's fashion periodicals and the refusal to acknowledge reform alternatives implicitly supported traditional dress. Clearly America, the land of pioneers and hardy frontiersmen who braved new territories and set new standards, offered no appropriate space for women's progressive change.

Peterson's Magazine

Peterson's, like *Sartain's,* highlighted the reform dress's "Americaness." *Peterson's* ignored the Bloomer until its October 1851 issue, a month later than its chief rivals. Like the others, this editor placed himself above the fray, insisting that his response came only because of numerous requests that the magazine address the issue. He insisted upon women's right to wear whatever they pleased, adding, "We have but little, however, to say about it." Nonetheless, in giving an opinion "only because it has been solicited!" *Peterson's* soundly renounced the costume, finding it less attractive than conventional dress and "frequently ugly," and cited the natural differences between men and women: "Nature has decided this matter, and there is no escaping Nature. A woman, in walking, moves the lower limbs with a circular sweep. A man moves them straight forward. This any anatomist will declare" ("Chit-Chat with Readers" *Peterson's* October 1851). The editor thus relied on the traditional argument of biology to oppose the dress, supporting naturally separate roles.[6]

Peterson's refused to believe the Bloomer was more convenient than conventional dress and, like other fashion periodicals, insisted on the superior beauty and convenience of a modified "flowing robe." The editor did suggest boots in winter, but such a token was typical of those who wished to appear concerned about women's health but who deliberately thwarted any real change. In November, noting the "deluge of communications" prompted by the October comments on the Bloomer, *Peterson's* printed a few letters from readers angered by or disagreeing with the magazine's stance. Accordingly, among its fashion plates for November, *Peterson's* presented two women dressed in Bloomer costumes—an evening dress and a walking dress (see fig. 3.6). The editor took the opportunity to point out *Peterson's* superiority to other fashion magazines because of its willingness to "cover the entire ground" of fashion, indicating the presentation was not supportive so much as responsive.

In December the magazine reminded readers of its status as a *World of Fashion* in its intention to carry "elegant plates of new Bloomer styles" as well as Paris fashions, and the January 1852 issue pictured another Bloomer evening dress. However, by April the editor apologized for carrying no Bloomer costumes since January, claiming that no new designs had appeared and pronouncing the costume a failure, "having seen no Bloomers in Philadelphia, New York, or Boston for several months." The periodical once again became silent on the issue. Although *Peterson's* appeared to make an effort to support the reform dress, the fashion magazines' editors and publishers

Fig. 3.6. Bloomer evening gown and walking dress, *Peterson's*, November 1851.

as a whole deliberately undercut efforts at dress reform. Of course, the magazines subsisted in great measure upon women's interest in elegant and complicated attire, perhaps one reason they used their influence to undermine the new dress. They also implicitly used assumptions that women edited the magazines to present the appearance that well-known and respected women found the change in dress distasteful.[7]

Graham's

Graham's, the Philadelphia periodical that came last to fashion promotion, provided the most direct attack on the Bloomer. This periodical ignored the reform dress until March 1852, when it printed a picture of the Bloomer first published in the *Lily.* Announcing the "Bloomer and all fresh from the newspaper and not credited to Paris" (332), the magazine offered a small representation, alone and looking despondent, next to Parisian fashions illustrating a woman and man together (see fig. 3.7). Bragging that its "Paris Fashions cost us $945 per month," a manner in which fashion magazines typically promoted the quality of the fashion plates they brought to readers, it noted also that its cost for producing the depiction of the Bloomer was $5. "Determined not to be outdone in generosity and to meet the views of the critics fully, we present 'the latest styles' as reported by Mrs. Bloomer 'expressly' for her own paper." Continuing the derision, the periodical noted, "It may be well to mention, by way of *description,* that the Bloomer is going to Church—as soon as she can get off from this dancing-party" (336). Thus *Graham's,* accustomed to locating women according to dress, insinuated the inappropriateness of the "public" dress for any other location.

Determining Who Speaks/Who Gets Heard

From the most prominent fashion magazines to those of general readership, the debate was over who had the right to speak and who would be heard with regards to rhetoric and to the specifics of women's dress. Clearly, reform women would not have the final say on dress. Many periodicals not explicitly fashion magazines also made efforts to reappropriate the conversation about dress and to reassert their rights to determine proper attire for women. Many had made discussions of women's dress a regular feature and clearly had no intention of relinquishing their authority on the subject. Self-proclaimed authorities on women's dress, such as magazine editors N. P. Willis and Genio Scott, added to the attack against the Bloomer. Scott lectured regularly on women's dress, and his *Mirror of Fashion* presented itself as an authority on the subject as well. Scott also served as fashion editor of the New York *Mirror.* Called "the great authority" on dress by the *Tribune,*

Fig. 3.7. The lonely Bloomer, *Graham's,* March 1852.

he ignored the attention garnered by the new dress during its early days. A proponent of women's apparel that offered "diaphanous tissues for overskirts, and gay colored silks with figured ornaments . . . resembling a flower garden," he continued to praise attire for women that could make one forget himself so that "you are surprised that the fragrance of the roses and pinks so much resemble modern perfumery" ("Mirror of Fashion"). However, by May, Scott acknowledged that women had decided to change the fashion and would do so. Still, he beseeched them to "confine their improvements to business and street wear, as to take away the full flowing skirts of the drawing-room would at once destroy half the poetry of human existence" ("The New Dress Question"). As such women as Elizabeth Oakes Smith, Harriet Austen, and Mrs. Cove Nichols began to lecture extensively in favor of the reform dress, Willis and Scott lectured widely in opposition to it.

Gleason's Pictorial Drawing Room Companion, noted for its illustrations, carried an illustration of the Bloomer in June 1851 drawn by a staff artist as a woman passed the *Gleason's* office. "The press have encouraged it because it is so bold and laughable," remarked the editor, but "public taste will soon condemn it" ("The Bloomer Costume" *Gleason's* 104). *Gleason's* regularly made comments on the Bloomer, but the most lengthy entailed the definition of the model Bloomer, which outlined the numerous traits of Bloomer wearers. According to this article, the model Bloomer loved the race track, left her children in the care of their father, fought with her fists, drank, smoked, and believed that women have been mistreated by men. "In short, the model Bloomer is a fast young woman in every respect, and it will not be for want of strenuous exertion that she does not revolutionize the world" ("The Model Bloomer" 423).

Editors also undermined the reform by deliberately misrepresenting women's purposes in creating the reform. The *Tribune* had claimed that Elizabeth Oakes Smith, in her lectures on dress, had simply called for shorter dresses. Despite letters from readers protesting that Smith had actually called for numerous reforms—simplification, elimination of corsets and tight lacing, modest coverage of arms and bodices—the *Tribune* continued to insist that a slight modification of traditional dress served the purposes of reformers at the same time that it retained elegance. Similarly, fashion magazines joined in weakening reformers' purposes even when they presented fashion plates of the Bloomer. Their representations denigrated efforts to abolish elaborate frills, to eliminate corsets and tight lacings, and to abolish the numerous and weighty petticoats that supported the voluminous skirts. The Bloomer dresses illustrated in the fashion magazines are as ornate and as tightly laced as dresses depicted in regular Paris fashion plates. In addition, although petticoats would have weighed less because of the shortened style, the dresses' skirts are obviously supported by numerous underskirts. When the fashion magazines did present illustrations of women in Bloomers, the women were always alone or with other women, while those presented in traditional European fashions were usually depicted accompanied by men (e.g., fig. 3.8). The message was clear that the dress was unattractive to men and that wearers would be isolated and castigated.

In addition to direct attacks and subtle disparaging of the reform dress in the manner of display, editors undermined the new dress by simple placement, often positioning negative accounts of Bloomers directly below glowing accounts of traditional feminine attire. For example, the *New York Daily Times* reported the many "Fine Ladies Promenading" Broadway on a pleasant morning after a succession of stormy days, noting, "You would have thought that church was just out" and elaborating on the predominance of blue and green silks on "the fashionable sidewalk as gay as a rainbow" (3). Both the tone and the associations with church and fine silks underscored what the headline led readers to accept—that these were "fine ladies."

Immediately below this report, readers learned of four Bloomers in the same location. "One of them was quite pretty, but her ungainly pantalets of purple linsey-woolsey were shocking. Another wore black silk, which was

Fig. 3.8. Parisian fashion plate, *Peterson's,* July 1851.

very pretty, but she herself was homely enough to turn milk sour" ("Lady Shangoes" 3). Thus, attacks came not only in direct opposition but also in the juxtaposition of positive images of fine ladies wearing traditional rainbow silks against one "homely" Bloomer and another wearing poor-quality linsey-woolsey, disparaging attempts at reform under the guise of objective reporting.

Regardless of widespread efforts to undermine the Bloomer and despite the backlash that greatly slowed the progress of reform in women's dress, steady efforts at change continued. Gattey claims, "By 1860, the Bloomer costume had been forgotten," to be "revived in England by Lady Harberton" in the late 1880s. However, the dress never lost its popularity with dress reformers. Amelia Bloomer's *Lily* had become extinct shortly after Bloomer sold the newspaper to move with her husband to Iowa. However, at about the same time, Lydia Sayer Hasbrouck initiated the *Sibyl,* the official organ of the Dress Reform Association, which held regular conventions for the promotion of dress reform.

In addition, with the popularity of bicycling and other sports in which women participated, various forms of bifurcated skirts became popular—all considered to be adaptations of the Bloomer. The enduring appeal of the Bloomer is evident as well in the continued use of the dress by cartoon-

Fig. 3.9. "The Bloomer Girl's Wedding," *Life,* May 1896.

ists. By the late nineteenth century, such popular periodicals as *Life* (see fig. 3.9) and *Harper's* relished depicting the New Woman's achievements with caricatures of bloomered women. For example, *Life* depicted the bloomered New Woman and her attendants as larger and more "masculine" than their male counterparts. Dress continued to be the visual representation of women's place and the primary focus for critics who feared and undermined change for women.

4

The Language of Passing and Desire: The Rhetoric of Cross-Dressing

[We] were all amused and disgusted . . . at the sight of a *thing* that nothing but the debased and depraved Yankee nation could produce. . . . She was dressed in the full uniform of a Federal Surgeon . . . not good looking and of course had tongue enough for a regiment of men. . . . She would be more at home in a "lunatic asylum."
—Confederate Captain Benedict J. Semmes, upon the capture of Dr. Mary E. Walker by Confederate soldiers, qtd. in Massey

*D*ress always delivered or supported messages for women, but while all dress "spoke" for wearers, none did so more explicitly than the deliberate cross-dressing that took place in the nineteenth century. Such dress spoke more strongly because it changed more profoundly the manner in which wearers were read. For many women, dress became the message, allowing for various forms of passing. If identities were fashioned according to bodies/clothing and the places/spaces those bodies were permitted to inhabit, clothing used for transgressing social, economic, racial, and gendered demarcations communicated for wearers in a manner that no other dress could. Quaker dress had spoken to the spiritual location of early women speakers, the Bloomer costume to the newly appropriated public space of women at midcentury. Women who chose to wear masculine clothing aligned themselves with a distinctively different place. But here the dress and appearance did not supplement the message but delivered it, specifically confounding normed roles for the purposes of passing (concealment) and enticing (display). Greater dangers were associated with this rhetorical undertaking, but wearers envisioned the possibility of far greater rewards.[1]

Representations in Literature

Nineteenth-century audiences were fascinated by notions of passing, especially across racial and gendered lines, and the literature is rife with such examples. Women characters often gain a measure of power by using dress to accomplish their purposes. Such rhetorical significance of dress is demonstrated in the century's best-known novel, Harriet Beecher Stowe's 1851 *Uncle Tom's Cabin,* in which characters cross race, class, and gender boundaries. Stowe gains sympathy for her slave characters by encouraging her white readers to identify with them, purposely demonstrating the similarity between black and white Americans. To that end, she creates primarily mulatto and quadroon slave characters whose skin coloring differs little from that of whites, and her characters exhibit strong Christian ideals. Moreover, Stowe emphasizes the dress of her light-skinned slaves, evoking the acceptable style of white middle-class Americans. Cassy, for example, despite her checkered background, is positioned to evoke empathy; like the presumed reader and despite her slave status, we find Cassy "dressed in neat and respectable garments" that embody white middle-class values (350). Other sympathetic characters—the slave mother and daughter, Susan and Emmeline—similarly wear the neat dress representative of their worth. Adolph and Rosa, the slaves of Augustine and Marie St. Clair, are similarly located according to dress.[2] In contrast, Stowe dresses her despicable slave trader Haley in gaudy, inappropriate dress, and Simon Legree shows his contempt for Tom as a human being by forcing him to exchange his middle-class "broadcloth suit, with well-starched linens and shining boots" for "a pair of old pantaloons and a dilapidated coat" and "a pair of course stout shoes" (335). Stowe thus highlights dress's ability to effectively demonstrate the similarities between the races, a dangerous likeness that led to sumptuary regulations in many of the slave states.

As Stowe demonstrates, dress so readily defines class, gender, and race that it may effectively allow for passing. In his escape from slavery, George has dressed himself in a gentlemanly manner, and he wears gloves that permit concealment of the "H" his master has branded into his hand in order to permanently identify him as a slave (112). His assumption of the persona of a well-to-do planter effectively renders a safe identity. And after her escape from Legree's plantation, Cassy dresses "after the manner of the Creole Spanish ladies" (421) in order to evade suspicions surrounding her journey out of slavery. Both cross racial and class boundaries by dressing the part. Gender roles can be transgressed as well. As Eliza and George make their final escape into Canada, Eliza changes her identity to that of a man simply by trimming her long hair, donning masculine clothing, and adopting a different manner of putting on her cloak. Her son, Harry, likewise becomes Harriet with a simple change of clothing.

Such fascination with dress and the transgressing of boundaries surfaces in much of the most popular fiction throughout the century. Women writers especially acknowledge the importance of dress both for demonstrating ethos and for passing. Early in the century, Catharine Maria Sedgwick demonstrated the importance of dress throughout her 1827 novel *Hope Leslie.* Dress serves to represent racial pride as well as to undermine dichotomous distinctions. The Pequod chief Mononotto rescues his son Oneco, who has been captured by settlers, and tears "from Oneco his English dress" (65) to reclaim his son's identity as a Pequod. Oneco's sister, Magawisca, sensitive to her own native heritage, refuses throughout the novel to change her attire from that of her own culture to the more acceptable English dress, even when she is on trial for her life and the change of clothing might help to sway jurors' feelings in her favor. Sedgwick's most memorable scenes, however, depict passing. When Magawisca is jailed by a patriarchal justice system with which Hope Leslie disagrees, Hope maneuvers her way into Magawisca's cell and dresses Magawisca in the clothing of her beloved tutor, Craddock, to facilitate Magawisca's escape. In this case Magawisca agrees to the strange attire, which does not compromise her integrity as a Pequod but rather permits her to circumvent and undermine an authority that treats individuals unfairly because of gender and race.

The novel is rife with such passing, and simply by modifying their dress characters change their identity, or at least the way they are read. Oneco successfully presents himself as a member of the Caucasian race to enter Governor Winthrop's home; by changing dress he masks his Indian identity. Sedgwick similarly portrays slippage in gender categories in her depiction of Rosa, the young French woman defiled by Sir Philip Gardiner. Rosa takes the gender-neutral name of Roslin and dresses as Sir Philip's page in order to mask the truth of their immoral and illegal relationship. In addition to the concealment, Rosa's dress provides her with the freedom of any young man to wander the streets alone at night and gives her access to places off-limits to young women. A simple change in clothing has provided liberation, both from spacial restrictions imposed on most women and from the ordinary scrutiny and condemnation visited upon women who break sexual taboos.

Perhaps the most famous fictional cross-dresser of the century was Capitola Black, heroine of E. D. E. N. Southworth's novel *The Hidden Hand.* Capitola assumes power generally denied to young women when she craftily changes clothes to suit her purposes. As a girl on the streets of New York, destitute, starving, and in danger of sexual molestation, Capitola dresses as a boy and handily supports herself with occupations normally unavailable to girls.

Southworth emphasizes the problems with gender stereotyping by high-lighting the repeated confusion among characters even after Capitola's sex has been recognized because she is still dressed as a boy. References to her continue to be muddled by everyone from the court recorder to a coach-man, even after her arrest. The coachman explains the arrest by referring to "a boy tuk up for wearing girl's clothes, or a girl took up for wearing boy's, I dunno which" (38). Similarly, the court clerk addresses Capitola, "Boy—*girl* I should say—what tempted you to put yourself into male attire?" (41). The recorder tells Capitola, "But my boy—*my good girl,* I mean—before you became so destitute, you should have found something or other to do" (43). These responses not only point to the confusion created by binary notions of sex based to such a large extent on appearance, but also high-light the unfairness of customs that deny women the privilege of support-ing themselves, since the reason Capitola cross-dresses is so that she *can* find something or other to do.

Major Warfield, who adopts Capitola, comforts her: "Come, come, my little man!—my good little *woman,* I mean—don't take it so to heart" (45). Only Capitola seems unconfused about her sexual identity. In fact, her only regret is that she had not thought of changing her appearance sooner be-cause, as she repeatedly confirms, "It was so easy" to change from a girl to a boy: "I went into that little back parlor *a girl,* and I came out *a boy,* with a suit of pants and jacket, with my hair cut short and a cap on my head!" (46).[3] Capitola's amazement at the ease with which she could gain the pro-tection and privileges afforded young men highlights the fascination that runs through much nineteenth-century American literature, especially that written by women. This captivation with clothing and its relation to place and privilege make for an interest in and facility for passing among social groups, across gender, and into public places normally reserved for white men of a certain class—an interest that surfaces constantly in the century's literature. By allowing their dress and appearance to speak for them, marginalized groups ably pass into entitlements denied them when they retain their original appearance.

The same interest in cross-dressing surfaces in the works of African Americans. As demonstrated in William Wells Brown's novel, *Clotel,* cross-dressing for slaves was tantamount with passing and often elided both gen-der and racial borders. Brown's protagonist, Clotel, exchanges clothing with George to allow for his escape from prison. Dressed in Clotel's clothing, George easily avoids detection and makes his escape to Canada. Clotel, simi-larly, dresses in men's clothing in her later escape from bondage as well as in her effort to rescue her daughter from slavery. As discussed in chapter 5, few African Americans cross-dressed for reasons other than passing. In their letters many demonstrate the necessity for disguise by wearing clothes different from those an enemy or authority might expect, but I have found no evidence of their calling attention deliberately to their bodies for the purpose of display. Nor have I found examples of black women speakers who cross-dressed. They more typically dressed very modestly and traditionally, even though they often acknowledged the necessity of passing for others. For example, Frances Ellen Watkins Harper wore modest dress appropriate to her gender when speaking, but in her letters she acknowledged her concern for others who disguised themselves in order to escape the bonds of slavery.[4] This abundance of cross-dressing in both fiction and daily life demonstrates the great interest in the slippage in categories of race and gender at a time when discussion about both categories was at its height.

Although the most popular fictional examples of passing occur within relatively acceptable cultural norms and represent an incident within a larger narrative, some works of fiction centered around the act of cross-dressing. In fact, so many either made this their major theme or in some way celebrated cross-dressing that Fannie Lee Townsend insisted that

> scarcely a novel is now written, in which the heroine is not made to figure in "a buff waistcoat with gilt buttons," or "a military frock buttoned to the chin." This is the spirit of the age; and it will result, unless seasonably checked, in the toleration, if not the sanction, of female pantaloonery. (179)

Townsend believed the most dangerous novel to be Jedediah Vincent Huntington's *Lady Alice; or, The New Una* (1849) in which "the reader not only excuses the beautiful heroine's disguise but cannot help admiring it"; the novel saw seven editions. Nearly equally dangerous were *Kate Darlington,* whose protagonist marries dressed in men's clothing; and *Fanny Campbell,* which depicts the exciting adventures at sea of Fanny, who is disguised as a sailor (179).[5]

Artistic Women

Such cross-dressing was not relegated to fiction. It became rather commonplace in the second half of the century. The reasons for women's dressing in men's clothing seem to be as diverse as artistic women demonstrating their interest in the avant-garde, to the need to escape slavery or maintain a safe presence (as demonstrated in the most popular novels), to an effort to promote dress reform and celebrity by individual speakers. The vogue created commotion and comment, and its origin was generally attributed to women artists, primarily writers and actresses, "amazons on the theatrical boards" (Townsend 178), especially to Helena Marie Weber.

Reporters and editors undoubtedly contributed to the fad by describing in detail and editorializing about Weber's philosophy and dress.[6] The Belgian author had written a pamphlet in which she recommended men's dress as "the most appropriate vesture for single females" (Townsend 178). Weber also insisted that men, in wearing bifurcated garments, had actually appropriated women's dress:

> The nether garment was first worn in the bifurcated form by the women of ancient Judah. How far it resembled the modern trowsers we have no definite information; but the fact is worth keeping in mind that women were the original wearers of trowsers. The exclusive claim which men so pertinaciously maintain to the use of this garment, is founded upon no principle of moral or social policy. It is an arbitrary claim, without a solitary argument to support it, not even that of prior usage. Nature never intended that the sexes should be distinguished by apparel. The beard which they assigned solely to man, is the natural token of the sex. But man effeminates himself, contrary to the evident purpose of nature, by shaving off his beard; and then, lest his sex should be mistaken, he arrogates to himself a particular form of dress, the wearing of which by the female sex, he declares to be a grave misdemeanor. ("Our Dress")

Weber's position may seem extreme for her time, but opponents feared Weber's wearing of men's dress because her example "rendered conspicuous by her great beauty and accomplishments, her irreproachable character and high social position, cannot fail to exercise a vast influence over those with whom she associates" (Townsend 178). Critics expressed greatest concern when examples were set by attractive, virtuous women—that is, those whose ethos exemplified the ideals of womanhood in other respects and were, therefore, most likely to attract admiration and imitation.

Called "champion of the forbidden attire" (Townsend 179), with her celebrated blue dress-coat, light buff waistcoat with gilt buttons, dark cravat, drab pants, and black silk hat, Weber became a model for young women. It was this example of a cross-dressing costume most often reported in newspapers across the country. Others of high visibility also wore men's attire. Fanny Kemble created a sensation with her escapades in and around Lennox, Massachusetts, attired in men's clothing ("Mrs. Kemble and Her New Costume" 94), and reporters marveled at tailors who acknowledged making pants for Anna Dickinson ("Trousers for Women" 5). Charlotte

Cushman attracted attention by wearing men's clothing for the theatrical roles she played, which seemed threatening enough, but she also sported masculine attire offstage.

Columnists

Popular women columnists and editors used their particular talents to capitalize on the notoriety surrounding women's use of masculine attire. Fanny Fern, popular columnist for the *New York Ledger,* took the opportunity to protest the arrest of women who wore men's clothing in two columns titled "A Law More Nice than Just." Fern cleverly depicted her own donning of her husband's clothing to take an evening walk during rainy weather. She criticized the "Miss Nancys" who insisted on the cultural customs and staid and unhealthy dress that restricted women needlessly:

> Think of the old maids (and weep) who have to stay at home evening after evening, when, if they provided themselves with a coat, pants and hat, they might go abroad, instead of sitting there with their noses flattened against the window-pane, looking vainly for "the Coming Man." Think of the married women who stay at home after their day's toil is done, waiting wearily for their thoughtless, truant husbands, when they might be taking the much needed independent walk in trousers, which custom forbids to petticoats. And this, I fancy, may be the secret of this famous law—who knows? It *wouldn't* be pleasant for some of them to be surprised by a touch on the shoulder from some dapper young fellow, whose familiar treble voice belied his corduroys. That's it, now. What a fool I was not to think of it—not to remember that men who make the laws, make them to meet all these little emergencies. (300)

Fern delighted in protesting men's laws that worked to women's detriment. Her use of humor here is typical of her style in pointing to inequities—a method that heightened her popularity and effectiveness.

Jane Grey Swisshelm also capitalized on the masculine dress sensation. As editor of the Pittsburgh *Saturday Visiter,* Swisshelm entered into repartee with George D. Prentice, editor of the *Louisville Journal,* after he praised her with the questionable remark, "She is a man all but the pantaloons." Swisshelm replied with the following poem:

> Perhaps you have been busy
> Horsewhipping Sal or Lizzie,
> Stealing some poor man's baby,
> Selling its mother, may-be.

You say—and you are witty—
That I—and, tis a pity—
Of manhood lack but dress;
But you lack manliness,
A body clean and new,
A soul within it, too.
Nature must change her plan
Ere you can be a man.

(qtd. in Woodward 68)

The keen battle of wits continued for eleven years, providing national coverage for Swisshelm. Swisshelm, who opposed even the Bloomer, of course disdained women who wore masculine dress. Nonetheless, she rarely missed an opportunity to parry with men who edited prominent periodicals, such as Prentice and N. P. Willis, who presumed to criticize and prescribe women's dress. She thus regularly appeared in print in many national publications.

Dr. Mary Walker

While numerous women dressed in men's clothing for a variety of rhetorical purposes, the woman public speaker who gained most notoriety for her masculine attire was Dr. Mary E. Walker. Dubbed "The Little Lady in Pants" by her biographer, Charles McCool Snyder, Walker began experimenting with dress by donning some bloomerlike pants while attending Syracuse Medical College. By the time she received a medical degree in June 1855, Walker had disposed of traditional feminine clothing entirely. She vacillated between a type of coat-dress modeled loosely on the Bloomer costume and traditional men's dress. When she married in 1856, she wore trousers and a coat-dress for the ceremony.[7] Walker became active in the dress reform movement almost immediately upon leaving medical school. In January 1857 she began writing for Lydia Sayer Hasbrouck's dress reform newspaper, the *Sibyl*, becoming one of its primary contributors, and by late 1857 she was lecturing publicly on dress reform (22). In 1860, in an effort to improve her public speaking, she attempted to enroll in a rhetoric class at Bowen Collegiate Institute but was denied admission because she was a woman. Women were just beginning to be admitted to institutions of higher learning, a major concession of masculine space to women. However, the added step of allowing women to prepare for the political place of the platform was typically denied women. Such opposition deterred neither Walker's determination to enter the class nor her public speaking. She joined a student debating society composed completely of men. Despite or, more likely, because of her wardrobe, the young men were intrigued. When the school suspended Walker for participating in debate, the young men in the debating society joined her in a march through the town in protest. The school responded by temporarily suspending the young men who participated in the protest and permanently suspending Walker (22).

Civil War Surgeon

When the Civil War broke out, Walker traveled to Washington to care for wounded soldiers. Controversy surrounded the efforts of a woman to act as surgeon, especially to soldiers. Walker further added to the debate by donning a blue officer's uniform with gold stripes down the pants, felt hat, and a green surgeon's sash, conflating the role and the dress that signified it. Participating in the traditional feminine capacity of nurturer to the sick, she nonetheless confounded that role by demanding her rights to act as surgeon, a role relegated to men. In addition, she sported men's clothing while simultaneously making a show of her long dark ringlets. Correspondents often reported on the mixing of gendered effects: "Dressed in male habiliments, with the exception of a girlish-looking straw hat, decked off with an ostrich feather, with a petite figure and feminine features, the *tout ensemble* is quite engaging" (qtd. in Woodward 284).[8] Reporters continued to find Walker "engaging" as long as she retained explicit features that marked her femininity. Later, when she cut or hid her long ringlets and removed all features of traditional feminine dress, she met with less patience.[9]

Walker offered her services to Confederate women and children and to the ill who lacked medical assistance.[10] Captured while riding behind enemy lines in 1864, she was incarcerated at Castle Thunder, a prison for political captives in Richmond, Virginia. Local newspapers reported the presence of the curious prisoner, noting her dress and her refusal to change it for one "more becoming to her sex" (Snyder 46); the epigraph at the head of this chapter illustrates the reaction of her Confederate captors. Similarly, when Major General William T. Sherman met Walker, he asked, "Why don't you wear proper clothing! That toggery is neither one thing or the other." He added, "Put on decent clothes . . . enter the hospitals where our boys are dying of wounds and fever, and imitate the example of women in hoops and petticoats, who are devoting their time to the work of nursing" (Spiegel and Suskind 219).

In 1866, in another traversing of traditional gender norms, Walker received the Congressional Medal of Honor for Meritorious Service, the only woman ever to have held this honor.[11] This, too, she wore each time she lectured, adding another striking feature to her appearance and enhancing an ethos that already received special recognition because of her clothing (see fig. 4.1). When Walker received a slightly altered replacement, instead of discarding or returning the replacement, she wore both medals. Years later, when she was no longer a celebrity, the Board of Medal Awards revoked her right to the medal and demanded that she return it, but Walker refused to do so and continued to wear the medal (Snyder 54).

Fig. 4.1. Dr. Mary Walker wearing dresscoat and pants and displaying her Congressional Medal of Honor. Courtesy of the Library of Congress.

Rhetoric Abroad

Later when Walker visited England, her clothing and appearance unquestionably contributed to the sensation she made there. She spoke on dress reform, woman's rights, and her experiences as a woman in a man's profession and in combat. According to Charles Snyder, she exhibited "little that was profound or original in her remarks." However, many newspapers lauded her rhetorical skills. The sensation she created, primarily because of her dress, contributed to her ability to draw large audiences nonetheless. The singular importance of her appearance to her audiences is noted more precisely by one of her promoters, who directed Walker to stay out of sight before her lectures: "If you walk about during day light, you can not expect people to pay for seeing you a second time. You must know that it is yourself that is the attraction and not the lecture" (A. Courtney, qtd. in Snyder 72). Thus, Walker spoke internationally with great celebrity and financial reward primarily because of the sensation she created by her masculine dress.

Although reviews of Walker's rhetorical effectiveness differ greatly, Walker herself sometimes felt that her skills were hampered by the rudeness of her audience. *All the Year Round* reported her concern at one of her stops in England:

> "You lose all the beauty of this lecture," said the doctor, irritated by the frequent interruptions to which she was subjected, "when you only allow me to say one or two words at a time; it is quite impossible but that the effect of what I have to say must be lost." ("M.D.")

The English also criticized her for succumbing to "the exceedingly florid nature of American oratory" that exhibited itself in such passages as "I had no Pillar of Fire to light me, no Jacob's Ladder by which to climb to my object, NO THAMES TUNNEL to pass under, NO ATLANTIC CABLE TO GO THROUGH" ("M.D."), but overall her speaking tour of England was highly successful.

When she visited Paris, attention again centered on her appearance. On a visit to the wards of the Hotel-Dieu,

> numbers gathered on her way to see what a confrere *en jupons* would look like. The peculiar costume of the lady added, of course, to the effect of the scene, and excited fresh curiosity. . . . She wore on her breast the medal received from Congress, and it is said (the *bout de l'orielle* of female vanity would peep out) that she took some care to show it off to advantage. (qtd. in Snyder 74)

For Walker, the purpose of masculine dress was not in passing unrecognized into another place. A supporter of woman's rights and dress reform, she insisted upon a woman's right to wear whatever attire she wished. She relished the mixing of gendered referents and deliberately demonstrated her ability to usurp space and clothing traditionally relegated to men, all the while displaying features that spoke to her femininity.

Some members of the press hinted at this. The *Spectator* mocked those in Walker's audiences who "profess[ed] to be slightly or greatly shocked" ("Dr. Mary Walker" 1305), implying that her sensation was based completely on her choice of dress. Noting Walker's poor rhetorical skills, the *Spectator* insisted that the real concern was not that Walker created confusion between the sexes: "Nobody took Dr. Mary for a man, or would have taken any woman similarly attired" (1305). The editorial contended that the real issue consisted in her dress being "condemned by the consensus of Western mankind," what it called an unfair opposition. Claiming that a woman's dress should be "always faintly enticing or fascinating," the editor defended Walker's right to wear the "rather long frock coat and black trousers, a hybrid costume in fact between that of a girl and that of a man," but disdained her because the "mannish" variety of clothing she sported failed to provide this function—one that positioned woman in a specific place and led to fulfillment of "woman's first function . . . to be mothers" (1305).

The dress propelled her into an upper-class society as well. Upon her return to England, one newspaper reported,

> She has just returned from a four week residence in Paris, where her costume attracted a large share of favorable notices. After being in public a few times she became so popular that she was constantly being invited to reunions of the best society. Her mission was brought under notice of the Empress, who appears to take considerable interest in the reformed dress, as communication between her Imperial Majesty and Dr. Walker tend to show." (qtd. in Snyder 75)[12]

While class stratification required a specific and strict adherence to dress codes, Walker's celebrity allowed her to breach class lines, if only for a short time.

Return to the United States

Walker's popularity continued upon her return to the United States. She toured on the lecture circuit and attended meetings for dress reform and woman's rights. She was highly successful at first. When the National Woman Suffrage Association met in Cincinnati, the audience insisted upon hearing from Walker after proceedings had come to an end. "The unique little lady in slabsided silks and elongated curls, tripped mincingly forward, and passing one pantalooned continuation behind the other, fetched a prim bow in acknowledgement of a perfect outburst of cheers and catcalls" (qtd. in Snyder 92). According to Snyder, "the Cincinnati papers gave her more attention than any of the other professionals at the convention" (93).

By the 1880s, Walker had discarded nearly all vestiges of feminine attire. She wore a man's coat and pants with silk top hat (see fig. 4.2). Beneath the coat she sported a man's shirt, collar, and tie. But the attire that helped to make her a celebrity had ceased to attract the kind of attention she desired. No longer young and attractive, with thin gray hair rather than the long ringlets that marked her femininity despite her dress, Walker came to be seen as merely eccentric. In addition, Walker lacked the acceptable feminine status highlighted by many other women speakers as they aged. She was unmarried, and she had never become a mother. Other successful speakers, such as Clarina Howard Nichols, who had divorced, had also remarried and borne children. Nichols wore acceptable matronly clothing, never the Bloomer, even though she defended the right of others to do so. She knitted openly while traveling to speaking engagements and waiting to speak. The childless Amelia Bloomer emphasized her happy marriage and devotion to home. She cared for children of relatives for long periods, and after moving to Iowa she adopted two who had been orphaned. Both carefully emphasized some feminine expectations for women when they challenged others. Walker made little effort toward such acknowledgments as she aged. As discussed in chapter 5, after midcentury, most women reformers abandoned dress that called attention to their breaching of norms. Having established their right to the political location defined by the platform, they hardly wished to draw further attention to their transgression of cultural spaces. They scorned Walker's radical dress. Reporters, too, seem to have grown tired of her and rarely acknowledged her except to point to her eccentricities.

Harassment

The rhetorical response to women who wore men's clothing depended to a great extent on the place they occupied and their station in life. Although they were most visible and performative when they assumed public stations such as the stage or the podium, in many respects those locations provided the greatest safety for them. The stage gave some protection to actresses Fanny Kemble and Helena Marie Weber, for example. And Dr. Mary Walker was never accosted while speaking publicly; however, she was repeatedly harassed by police officers upon the street. On 5 June 1866, a police officer

Fig. 4.2. Dr. Mary Walker
in the 1880s. Courtesy of
the Library of Congress.

tried to arrest her on Canal Street in New York City. She wore a "long coat
or robe and a pair of cloth pants," and according to the *New York Times,* a
police officer "imagining that there was something wrong about this, and
that a lady ought not to be allowed to dress as she pleases," took her to the
police station. She was there arraigned by a sergeant who threatened to "lock
her up instantly." Walker warned him that she was well known and that
she had been awarded the Congressional Medal of Honor. The sergeant
grudgingly dismissed her, but the indignant Dr. Walker warned him that
he would be called to answer for his conduct by the police commissions
on the next day ("Unauthorized Arrest" 8).

Although charges against her were always dismissed, Walker was repeatedly subjected to the jeers and taunts of men in authority. Reports suggest
that her arrests were a form of purposeful harassment, and newspapers

delighted in presenting the incidents, often on the front page. The problem seems to be that she had abandoned all attempts to appear feminine. Typically, reports focused on Walker's masculine language as well as her dress, depicting her sarcastic repartee and contributing to the mocking tone. For example, when she was arrested in Chicago, the *New York Times* described her as "sauntering" in front of the arresting officer and saying "things with emphasis." When the officers at the station greeted her statements "with smiles and chuckles," she produced a letter from Congress "that has given me permission to wear men's clothing. Here is the document—if you are able to read, which I doubt" ("Dr. Walker Arrested Again"). On the occasion of another arrest, the *Times* reported her "saucy response" and her suggesting that the arresting officer "go along and mind his own business." The account quoted Walker as saying, "I'll carry a pistol and I'll use it if ever I'm interfered with again" ("Dr. Mary Walker Arrested"). In blatantly ignoring expectations for quiet, self-effacing and reticent women, Walker drew ridicule.

All of Walker's harassment was not at the hands of the police. In October 1913, a band of young men arrived at her home, knocked on the door, and told her that her barn was afire. When Walker stepped from her home, she found the young men had "a kettle of tar and a feather pillow" with which to tar and feather her. Although they tried to catch her, Walker ran quickly back into the house, locked the door, and phoned the police. She was nearly eighty-one years old at the time ("Tar for Dr. Mary Walker").

Later generations have exhibited greater appreciation for Walker. President Carter restored her Congressional Medal of Honor. Similarly, in 1982, the U.S. Postal Service issued a postage stamp to commemorate the 150th anniversary of her birth (see fig. 4.3). Ironically, the depiction is one with which Walker would have been incensed. The designer, Glenora Case Richards, "chose to emphasize the femininity of her subject" by portray-

Fig. 4.3. Dr. Mary Walker
postal stamp, issued 1982.

ing her in "a dark Victorian dress brightened by a white collar and a jabot of frilly lace cascading down the front" rather than in the masculine attire Walker would have insisted upon (Tower).

Rewards and Punishment: Social Connections and Cultural Expectations

While celebrities such as Walker might be excused for unusual dress, general disapproval met those without such renown except in cases where they dressed in men's apparel for "good" reasons, as when they acted on sanctioned cultural norms. When women wore such clothing for unconventional purposes, however, they were treated badly by the press, police, and judges. The extent of harassment also depended largely on social and economic means. Cross-dressing, more than any other type of dress, encouraged or tempered harsh reactions according to class. Those without well-connected friends or family members able or willing to come to their rescue were often remanded to prison. For example, the Philadelphia *Public Ledger* reported approvingly of a young woman who dressed in men's apparel in order to travel safely from Philadelphia to Pittsburgh to seek help for her father. The father had been imprisoned for another person's debt. When her identity was discovered at a public house, "she was kindly furnished with proper clothing" and helped to reach home. With approbation, the newspaper reported:

> Such an example of filial affection in a young and delicate female, used to all the refinements of society, cannot be too much admired. Her disguise was assumed for the purpose of securing her personal safety during her journey—a journey of something like 600 miles, undertaken solely with the hope of liberating a father from prison. ("A Young Lady Dressed in Male Apparel" 2)

The young woman was "used to all the refinements of society" and exhibiting "filial affection." Without her father or other masculine protector, she necessarily needed to find other means of protection, a means allowable only in highly unusual situations because young women were expected to have protectors. Her behavior was excusable, even laudatory, since her presumed protector was imprisoned. All these rationales supported and confirmed women's subordination to men and their need for masculine protectors.

On the other hand, those worthless enough to have no connection to traditional guardians seemingly deserved little protection from other patriarchal authorities. Local law enforcers who felt they must assume authority for containing and policing behavior that deviated from the norm often reacted with physical hostility to cross-dressers; poor women who had no influential connections or wealth often found themselves imprisoned for their escapades. For example, New Yorker Jennie F. Westbrook, alias Frank De Nyce, or Frank D. Chester, found herself the subject of a Supreme Court case and repeatedly imprisoned. In February 1882 she was sentenced to prison for six months because she "had personated a man by wearing men's clothing." Westbrook claimed she had assumed the clothing simply to "procure a better living than she could if she wore feminine robes" ("The Woman Who Wore Men's Clothes" 3). While such an honorable cause sanctioned cross-dressing for many fictional characters, Westbrook's transgression of cultural roles by dressing in men's clothing, in seeking employment outside women's normal places of employment, and in suggesting an ambitious desire to better herself through her own skills rather than through marriage found little compassion among police authorities.

The New York Supreme Court dismissed the charge, claiming that simply wearing men's clothing was not a crime; upon her release, however, Westbrook was immediately rearrested for perjury and committed to the Tombs ("The Woman in Trousers" 3). Arrested again in November 1883, she received an impatient reprimand from the *New York Times* for her failure to reform despite the "mistaken sympathy wasted upon her by several respectable but impressionable ladies" after her previous arrests ("Arrested Again in Male Attire" 3). The officers and newspapers refused to permit her to speak for herself, basing interpretations on the language of her dress alone, reading her character through her dress and determining it to be questionable. Defending what the newspaper obviously considered justifiable detention, the officer claimed to have watched her for several weeks "in and about saloons and questionable resorts" and assumed that the "male attire was for improper purposes" (3). She was again dismissed because she had worn no mask and made no attempt to disguise her features, but the newspaper described her "ill-fitting" clothes and explained that she had been arrested as she smoked a cigar. Westbrook's arrests were unquestionably related to her occupation of places denied women—saloons and dubious resorts—and to the wearing of clothing that permitted her to do so. Men's clothing, especially loose-fitting clothing that allowed her to hide the corporeal features defining her sex, gave her entry into locations, and to practices, such as smoking phallic cigars, that she was unlicensed to enjoy because she was a woman.

Emma Snodgrass

Boston, too, had its cross-dressers, the most famous being Emma Snodgrass. In December 1852, the *Herald* reported on eight episodes where women were arrested for wearing men's clothing. The rhetoric that accompanies such descriptions suggests a license for desire associated with women who defied traditional norms—perhaps a release of the suppression surrounding nineteenth-century pretensions about passive "proper" women that restricted normal expressions of sexual desire. Ironically, the confusion surrounding attitudes toward such women connected seemingly contradictory claims about the "unsexed" nature of such women with a rhetoric that exposes the enticement and allure observers felt. On 31 December, the *Herald* reported:

> Since the peculiarities of Emma Snodgrass have become so familiar to the public, the custom of ladies promenading the streets in coat and pants is getting to be rather common. Almost any evening some of these unsexed individuals may be seen in Washington street creating a sensation among romantic loving young men. ("Donning Male Attire" 4)

The contradictory message here that women dressed in coats and pants became unsexed yet created a sensation among romantic young men demonstrates the confusion that obvious cross-dressing created, coupling disdain with desire.

For the most part, women who thus appeared in men's clothing could be treated kindly and in good humor if the breech in decorum appeared to be a solitary lark. If women feigned modesty, authorities simply reprimanded them. In one reported case, the cross-dresser resorted to a display of femininity; she was accompanied by a man, conducted herself "with propriety," confessed her transgression, and pleaded with the official in charge to protect her anonymity—all acceptable feminine behavior. Such women were generally dismissed into the care of their escorts:

> A young lady of romantic disposition and "highly respectable connections" visited the Howard Athenaeum on Monday evening, dressed in male attire. Her pretty face of "sweet sixteen" attracted much attention—too much for her modesty, and she hastily retired. ("A Young Lady of Romantic Disposition" 4)

In this case the "lady" is read as having romantic notions about dress, no doubt a reading enabled by her membership in a well-connected family. Her modesty also demonstrates a femininity that allows for a "romantic" reading of her character. Similar readings surfaced repeatedly:

> The desire on the part of young women to don the pantaloons appears to be on the increase. A young girl residing in Roxbury, a few

evenings since appeared in the principal street of that city, attired in male apparel. She was accompanied by a friend. Together they visited several of the saloons in the precinct. The young woman otherwise conducted herself with propriety, and when she was detected in her male dress, at once owned up to the gallant bachelor police officer, whose attention was called to her in the street. The officer did not take her in charge, but sent her home, after she promised not to appear again in other than female apparel. The eccentric girl entreated that she should not be exposed, and the officer promised not to divulge her name.—Should she reappear in her male dress, we shall give her name and romantic history. ("Another Damsel in Pants" 4)

The "romantic" suggestions behind attention to these young women confirms conventional attitudes. The language, in one sense, relegates women to an ethereal sphere that belies the sexual realities of their bodies and the men's desire to appropriate and make use of them. Even such language reserved for "proper" young cross-dressers of a certain class reveals an acknowledgment of desire for such women, however. In proper patriarchal manner, too, the newspaper's threat to release information if the young woman does not respond according to patriarchal definitions of the appropriate is telling. The surface chivalrous protection of the naive and weak by authorities exposes a threat to reveal the concealed—a double entendre for women who have done just that by baring the slippery and superficial facade behind dichotomous notions about the two sexes. The final solution is to remove women from locations they should not occupy and return them to their proper places under the confinement and authority of their fathers or other authority figures, who will ensure their proper dress according to defined gender roles.

Although Boston's Emma Snodgrass repeatedly appeared in men's clothing, she escaped imprisonment primarily because her father was an assistant captain in the New York Police Department. Snodgrass flaunted not only her penchant for men's attire but also her disdain for modesty and patriarchal authority. The *Herald* reported on Snodgrass's activities five times within two and a half weeks. The newspaper noted her visits to places of amusement around Boston ("Emma Snodgrass" 15 December), the attraction of her pants and frock coats for "romantic young men . . . seeking acquaintance with her" ("Emma Snodgrass" 18 December), and the "profound sensation" she created in a trip to Portsmouth, New Hampshire ("Emma Snodgrass" 22 December). In late December, she was arrested by "a veteran police officer" who removed her from a place properly attended by women only when accompanied by a man:

> Emma, when arrested, was pursuing her way from the popular sa-
> loon of Col. Wheelcock, in Court Square, where she has occasion-
> ally dined. Emma is fashionably dressed—wears a heavy oversack, a
> fancy cap, high heeled boots, a faultless dickey, and straw-colored
> gloves. ("Emma Snodgrass" 29 December)

In an editorial responding to the cross-dressing, the newspaper noted that
"the young female had for the last two or three months been the subject of
many newspaper paragraphs, and has attracted the attention of all the grave
and gay, young and old men, of our metropolis" ("Emma" 2).

With no legal statutes to deal with such infringements on women's expected behavior, authorities had permitted Snodgrass free movement. Finally, their patience ended. Still, problems surfaced when the justice system tried to deal with this oddity. Snodgrass was charged with vagrancy,
"accused of wandering about from place to place, without means of support" ("Movements of Emma Snodgrass" 7). She had been arrested twice
previously, once at the request of her father, as a runaway from his home;
she pleaded reasonable age and difficulties within her father's household.
The second arrest had been for wearing men's apparel, but since no laws
existed permitting such an arrest, this attempt was unsuccessful as well.
Finally, efforts to prove that Snodgrass was a vagrant failed; government
witnesses testified to her public appearance in men's attire, but all other
witnesses verified her financial stability and reported her timely payment
of all bills.

> She was then taken into the Judge's Room, where she received some
> good advice from his Honor relative to resuming the habiliments of
> her sex and returning to her father's house, which she promised to
> do. ("Movements of Emma Snodgrass" 7)

As the newspaper noted, "the city officials have been somewhat puzzled as
to the means of putting a stop to her proceedings" ("Movements" 7). The
New York Herald reported Snodgrass's return to New York on 3 January ("We
Understand" 7); later she was tried on a charge of vagrancy in New York.
The complaint was not sustained, and she was discharged ("The Young Lady
in Pants" 3).

Legal Confusion

Women's and men's roles and dress were firmly dichotomized by the mid-
nineteenth century. Anne Fausto-Sterling has discussed "the political weight
our culture places on ascertaining a person's correct 'sex'" and the deep
confusion "surrounding persons and situations where it is not easily deter-

mined" (301). Conventions about place only added to the perplexion. Women who cross-dressed but accompanied a man were harassed less because expectations for place had not been disrupted. But women were categorized by place as well as dress, and when "good" women appeared in locations that only prostitutes or "streetwalkers" frequented without an escort, the apprehension was magnified. As authorities determined that arrests based on clothing were illegal, they turned immediately to laws based on place, charging women with vagrancy and suggesting the unlawfulness of their being without a home or domestic location—of being out of place— of roaming the streets without one licensed to occupy that space. Operations premised on easily recognized differences added both consternation and anger because authorities were unprepared to address such infractions. Conventions surrounding women's dress and place were so strong that legislators had failed to envision the need for such laws, and although some women might be arrested for vagrancy or for disorderly conduct, women better positioned presented substantial problems for authorities.

Hence, municipalities did occasionally pass ordinances against crossdressing in public. San Francisco passed such a law in the 1860s, but when Eliza Hurd De Wolfe was arrested, her attorney argued that the board of supervisors had no authority to pass such a law because no state or common law forbade it. The judge ruled against her, arguing that a woman could not wear men's clothing "if her dress tended to excite a mob" ("A Question of Dress in San Francisco" 2). Given the nature of previous responses to cross-dressed women, the word *excite* is an interesting word choice perhaps, a barely clothed insinuation of desire.

Authorities sometimes detained young women on the pretense of protection. New York authorities arrested Mirriam Kirkpatrick, a young Scottish woman of nineteen, when she arrived from Canada, detained her overnight, and then placed her in the care of a prison matron to remain until "friends" could be notified ("A Female in Breeches" 7). In other instances, such as that of Mary Clements, women might be charged with disorderly conduct, in which case the women generally assumed modest and repentant attitudes in order to be released, often after the judge's "severely reprimanding her . . . she promised never again to be guilty of a similar offense" ("A Female in Pantaloons" 7). Cross-dressing made such determinations difficult.

While such attention to dress measured and punished deviation from assigned roles and places, it also exposed and undermined the assumed "natural" dichotomies of sex and race dependent primarily on visual attribution. For a culture that relied so heavily on external appearance, the increased attention to cross-dressing interrogated numerous underlying cultural assumptions. The very ease with which women altered images questioned the legitimacy of the dichotomies on which appearances were based. As Amy Robinson suggests, "The 'problem' of identity . . . is predicated on the false promise of the visible as an epistemological guarantee" (716). For women activists, revelations of the inadequacy of that guarantee exposed the slippage inherent in nineteenth-century notions about sex, lending support to women's changing roles and locations.

For women public speakers, cross-dressing's contribution to rhetorical effectiveness was mixed. The *Sibyl* was moderately successful, and women dress reformers, especially those associated with the National Dress Reform Association, continued to speak on a regular basis before respectably sized audiences and to receive some press coverage. However, with the exception of Dr. Mary Walker, the most successful speakers dressed in acceptable feminine styles, continuing or returning to the traditional, if slightly shortened, skirt with fewer petticoats. They abandoned bifurcated garments until the popularity of the bicycle and the rage of the new woman made split garments popular once again. Even Walker's success based on cross-dressing was precarious. As she aged and lost or eliminated signs of her femininity, both her acceptance and rhetorical effectiveness were diminished.

5

[Re]Fashioning a Proper Image by Dressing the Part

The modern tendencies in the art of expression are to the closest
naturalness attainable without flatness, to suggestiveness rather than
to literal expressiveness, and to hold to the exact truth in preference
to any scheme of decorative beauty.
—Anna Morgan, "The Art of Elocution," 1893 Woman's Congress

*M*uch as early women speakers had distanced themselves from Frances
Wright and her radical attire, most women making public appearances after midcentury distanced themselves from the Bloomer and other forms of
extreme dress. While many saw the desertion of the reform dress as capitulation, it represented also the greater sanction of women speakers and a
deliberate rhetorical strategy on their part to present a favorable ethos for
gaining approval for themselves as speakers and for their ideas. Whereas
earlier critics had focused on dress and appearance as a means of discredit-
ing publicly active women, women speakers' dress later in the century became a means by which women sought favorable coverage, and audiences,
especially newspaper reporters, provided it. In the focus on appearance,
however, issues of class and race became conspicuously pronounced.

Abandoning the Short Dress

The Bloomer had successfully drawn audiences to hear women speakers,
garnering attention for their causes. For many women—Jane Grey Swisshelm, Susan B. Anthony, and Lucy Stone—the dress had furthered a national, and for Amelia Bloomer herself an international, reputation. But
the novelty faded, and the strain of family and public opposition led most
reformers to abandon the Bloomer. According to Ida Harper, the women
who wore Bloomers were not only constantly harassed by strangers but

alienated from families and friends as well: "Their husbands and children refused to be seen with them in public, and they were wholly ostracized by other women. . . . Mrs. Bloomer wore the costume eight years, but very few held out one-fourth of that time" (114). Elizabeth Cady Stanton apparently stopped wearing the Bloomer after two or three years because "the pressure brought to bear upon her by her father and other friends was so great, that she finally yielded to their wishes and returned to long skirts" (D. C. Bloomer 70). Shortly after Stanton had "capitulated," Anthony abandoned the dress as well (Harper 115); however, Anthony struggled with her decision more than other reform leaders. Although publicly the women often claimed they relinquished the dress "for the cause,"[1] in their private letters to one another they spoke primarily of freedom from emotional strain.

Stanton wrote Anthony, "I know what you must suffer in consenting to bow again to the tyranny of fashion, but I know also what you suffer among fashionable people in wearing the short dress; and so, not for the sake of the cause, nor for any sake but your own, take it off! We put it on for greater freedom, but what is physical freedom compared with mental bondage?" (Harper 115). Stone also wrote Anthony:

> Dear Susan,
>
> About the dress, it is all fudge for anybody to pretend that any cause that deserves to live is impeded by the length of your skirt. I know, from having tried through half the Union, that audiences listen, and assent, just as well to one who speaks truth in a short as in a long dress. No, no, Susan, it is all a pretense that the cause will suffer. I am annoyed to death by people who recognize me by my clothes, and when I get a seat in the cars, they will get a seat by me and bore me for a whole day with the stupidest stuff in the world. Much of that I should escape if I dressed like others. Then again, when I go to a new city, where are many places of interest to see, and from which I could learn much, if I go out a horde of boys pursue me and destroy all comfort. Then, too, the blowing up by the wind, which is so provoking, when people stare and laugh. (Blackwell 107–8)

Despite these problems, Stone wore the dress for nearly four years. Because she felt traditional clothing placed "women in bondage" (109) and because of her "own greater comfort in the short dress" (110), she hesitated to give up the Bloomer. But, finally, recognizing that the dress had gained a voice she could not control, she decided to supplement her wardrobe with a long dress (112), and Anthony then felt able to acquiesce, too: "If Lucy Stone, with all her reputation, her powers of eloquence, her loveliness of character that wins all who once hear the sound of her voice, cannot bear the martyrdom of the dress, who, I ask, can?" (112).

Steadfast dress reformers felt betrayed. They particularly resented Stone's return to long skirts because she had been unwavering in her support of the reform dress. Lydia Sayer Hasbrouck expressed her dismay in the *Sibyl:*

> She has not only injured the cause, but she has caused the mass to look upon her as lacking in the true, strong elements that should constitute a reformer. . . . We know the course she now takes has robbed her of much influence, both with dress reformers and every other true and unflinching reformer. It deeply pains us. . . . She, the embodiment of strength, has been held up to us so often we wish to let the world know that our strength is not from her. ("Lucy Stone's Position" 540)

Regardless of charges of capitulation against early dress reformers and despite the adamant adherence to dress reform of such women as Hasbrouck, most reform leaders readily moved beyond radical dress toward the mainstream, intent on creating a favorable ethos that might further their causes. Few women in the major reform movements wore dress traditionally assigned to men; as noted in chapter 4, Dr. Mary Walker was atypical, even derided by major figures in the movements for impugning the cause for women by dressing as a man.

A major factor contributing to reform leaders' attitudes about dress derives from the gradual acceptance of women's public place. While still facing opposition, women speakers were no longer an anomaly, and the growing women's organizations had little trouble ensuring either adequate attendance or press coverage for major meetings. The largest organizations thus shifted their focus toward attaining positive press and constructing a favorable image of the public woman. Aware of the close relationship between their appearance and public acceptance, leaders of most women's organizations encouraged members to dress in "acceptable" fashion. The press responded: Instead of detailing dress to denigrate speakers, attention to dress became a means for praising and seeking acceptance for most women speakers, especially white middle-class women. The greater the celebrity, the more attention to details of dress. For black women speakers, however, audiences seemed able to focus little attention on dress or appearance beyond complexion. Black-owned newspapers and those especially supportive of racial acceptance might focus on the "proper" attire of a black speaker in order to demonstrate her "ladylike" qualities, but most newspapers and listeners focused attention on complexion.

African American Women and the Bloomer

Complexities of dress for black women were coded differently from those of white women. While white women reform leaders were adopting the Bloomer, black reform leaders, such as Sojourner Truth and Frances Ellen Watkins Harper, retained more customary dress. Busy with other pressing needs and aware of problems in drawing attention to bodies that already held negative connotations in nineteenth-century America, black women rarely adopted unusual or radical attire. In addition, well-to-do blacks often "regarded bourgeois decorum as an important emancipatory cultural discourse" (Tate 4). As Shirley Logan notes, while black women wanted to assist "personal and racial uplift," they also wanted to "argue black women into the cult of true womanhood" (*We Are Coming* 112). As noted in chapter 3, so alien was the notion of black women's assuming the Bloomer that young men sometimes presented poor black women with Bloomer costumes in order to ridicule both ("A Colored Lady"). Sojourner Truth dismissed the Bloomer as too closely resembling clothing she had been forced to wear during her years of slavery. According to Harriet Beecher Stowe, Truth gave the following account of her disaffection for the Bloomer:

> "Some on 'em came round me, an' asked why I didn't wear Bloomers. An' I told 'em I had Bloomers enough when I was in bondage. You see," she said, "dey used to weave what dey called nigger-cloth, an' each one of us got jes' sech a strip, an' had to wear it width-wise. Them that was short got along pretty well, but as for me"—She gave an indescribably droll glance at her long limbs and then at us, and added,—"Tell you, I had enough of Bloomers in them days." ("Sojourner Truth" 479)

For Truth, the Bloomer represented a form of bondage.

On the other hand, Harriet Tubman found the Bloomer physically liberating, but not for public purposes. As Tubman tells it, during the famous Combahee River raid during which she led so many slaves to freedom,

> I was carrying two pigs for a poor sick woman, who had a child to carry, and the order "double quick" was given, and I started to run, stepped on my dress, it being rather long, and fell and tore it almost off, so that when I got on board the boat, there was hardly anything left of it but shreds. I made up my mind then I would never wear a long dress on another expedition of the kind, but would have a *bloomer* as soon as I could get it. (Conrad 176–77)

Tubman's letter requesting "a *bloomer* dress, made of some coarse, strong material to wear on *expeditions*" (177) was written in 1863 and suggests her need for a bifurcated garment that would not impede her movement. Although Earl Conrad suggests that Tubman's use of the Bloomer was intended to impress her woman suffragist friends, those reformers would have long ago abandoned the costume, and there is no evidence that Tubman ever wore Bloomers in public. Her use of the dress was almost assuredly practical. By contrast, nearly all black women who appeared publicly in the nineteenth century dressed carefully so as to diminish attention to their difference and to avoid further impugning their character.

The Woman's Christian Temperance Union

Most public women in the latter part of the century sought to enhance their ethos by presenting an "appropriate" appearance. The most effective group at presenting a proper image and at gleaning positive press was the Woman's Christian Temperance Union (WCTU). The Woman's Crusade, precursor to the WCTU, provides ample evidence of women's awareness of dress's impact on how they were perceived. Annie Wittenmyer, one of the leaders of the Woman's Crusade and first president of the WCTU, describes members' attention to dress. She notes the jeers associated with dress and place: "Go home, old woman, and mend your husband's breeches" and "Go home and darn your stockings" (30). When charged with disorderly conduct for their march on local saloons, the crusaders dressed carefully for their court appearance: "We put on all our best things, and though I say it, were FORTY-THREE OF THE PRETTIEST WOMEN YOU EVER SAW" (241). According to Wittenmyer, officials were disarmed, "told us we had been naughty," and forgave the women. Wittenmyer's capitalization of the particular section dealing with appearance demonstrates her awareness of the importance of dress for public women, a concern that continued when the women formed the WCTU in 1874.

By far the largest organization of women in the final quarter of the century, the WCTU actively sought to influence press reportage. Leaders organized and taught members to provide prepared copy for newspapers and, most significantly for this discussion, the women appropriated the very emphasis on appearance that had been problematic for some earlier speakers. Inverting the sign of women's fragility, they enlisted "feminine" dress as a powerful rhetorical symbol of their stations and characters that helped to equalize the strong visual presence that men had been able to assume throughout the century. Such attention to appearance, especially with regards to the WCTU, changed early press focus on the "manly" or "masculinized" speaker to descriptions of the "womanly" rhetor, a depiction that disarmed critics.

From its inception, the organization deliberately strove for good press coverage. Beginning with the first meeting of the national organization, leaders had reserved front row seats for reporters and were careful to thank them publicly for "the patience manifested during the sittings, and for the correctness and fidelity with which they reported the proceedings" (*Minutes* 1874, 39). The WCTU "Plan of Work" as outlined in the 1874 *Minutes* exhibits further evidence of their awareness of the importance of the press, stating as one purpose "in all possible ways enlisting the press in this reform" (25). Eventually, the organization established a standing committee of six women, "On Influencing the Press," later a department that continued throughout the century. Composed of some of its most influential members, the department labored vigorously to ensure positive reporting of WCTU activities.

Members carefully avoided dress that might in any way impugn their organization, enlisting dress as the signifier of the "womanly" rhetor. The primary goal of Frances E. Willard, president of the WCTU during most of the nineteenth century, was to convince the average woman of the need to become politically active in favor of women's needs. Leaders discouraged extremes and encouraged moderation. They advised members that the purpose of dress was to conceal, to protect from the weather, and to suggest rather than to define the shape, especially shaping by means of corsets and other binding paraphernalia. The dress also functioned rhetorically to conceal or diminish appearances of undue political fervor, protecting members from ridicule and dismissal.

Willard even had appropriate clothing designed specifically for WCTU members (see fig. 5.1). Accompanying an advertisement for the Willard Dress, Annie Jenness Miller's "Art in Dress" commentary praised "careful attention to distinct principles in dress" and wondered at the minority who "regard dress as a trivial and unimportant question," much as women's other cares and concerns were regarded. Miller clearly equated women's dress with ethos:

> Dress is all important, for it marks the refinement of character as unmistakably as does the behavior or conversation; and, for this reason, those of us who are interested in the art of dressing believe in the ultimate triumph of what is correct and symmetrical. In the future more, and not less, attention will be paid to dress, and by dress I mean clothing the body so that the integrity of natural functions shall be considered in connection with picturesque effect. ("The Willard Dress")

The Willard Dress.

The Dress was designed
especially for members
of the

W. C. T. U.

at the request of

MISS FRANCES WILLARD,

and members ordering it will
receive a free pattern of the
divided skirt.

Price of Willard Pattern, 50 Cents.

THE
JENNESS MILLER PUB. CO.,
17 W. 125th Street, New York.

Fig. 5.1. The Willard Dress. Courtesy of the Frances E. Willard Memorial Library and the National Woman's Christian Temperance Union, Evanston, Illinois.

"Correct" dress continued to be a concern for temperance women. As another means of presenting a proper ethos in dress, leaders encouraged members to wear their Union badge, a white ribbon that symbolized purity and peace.

The Press and the WCTU

Press coverage was usually positive for the WCTU. Reporters often associated the organization with morality and organized religion. When Baltimore hosted the national convention in 1878, the *Baltimore and American Commercial Advertiser* reported:

> Persons passing on the leading streets and riding in the street cars yesterday must have met groups of ladies who looked like strangers in the city, and who also bore unmistakable evidences of belonging to some semi-religious body. Some wore simple drab and the small white-frilled Quaker bonnets, others were tall and clad in somber traveling suits looking severely Puritanical, and more again were richly but yet tastefully attired in silk dresses and subdued bonnets, such as suited serious-minded ladies not very juvenile in years. ("Religious" 4)

To ensure that readers understood the solemn purpose of the group, the writer emphasized the tasteful but sober attire and the maturity of members. Such dress would have provided an ethical persona acceptable to audiences, one conducive to serious attention to the speaker.

The positive press for the WCTU extended especially to its second president, Frances E. Willard. Of all reform leaders in the final part of the century, the press gave the greatest and most favorable attention to Willard. Perhaps the best-known and most admired American woman of the nineteenth century and often credited with much of the success of the WCTU, Willard was especially adept at presenting rhetorically effective images. Along with her closest allies, she carefully constructed her own positive image. Correspondence between Willard's personal secretary, Anna A. Gordon, and Willard's mother attests to the concern of all three that Willard appear appropriately dignified. Their letters discuss the amounts and styles of lace for Willard's dress, for example, representing their wishes that Willard look adequately fashionable and feminine but in no way showy. Similarly, in a pamphlet for the Social Purity series entitled "Dress and Vice," Willard made clear that "early in my temperance apostleship" she had "discarded corsets and high heeled shoes . . . and adopted a more hygienic way of living in nearly all regard" (10), and she encouraged such reform in WCTU members: "Criticism upon the habits of our brothers come with poor grace from those whose own sins against God's laws written in their members fill as many graveyards as do the tobacco and alcohol habits" (10).

Willard's personal dress and appearance always drew reassuring commentary from reporters. During the 1884 convention in St. Louis, for example, the *Post-Dispatch* described her as

> a slight, delicate middle-aged lady, [who] wears her light brown hair brushed smoothly down over her temples. She dresses very plainly but tastefully, in subdued colors. No one can look at her clear, resolute eyes without feeling that the glasses she wears are entirely for use and not at all for ornament. Jewelry is not a weakness of hers, and a pretty little gold watch that peeps out from her waist pocket is the only thing of this kind visible. ("Notable Women" 2)

Willard's simple hairstyle and natural complexion, along with her modest dress and her eschewing of flashy or elaborate decoration, increased her credibility, preparing audiences to hear and be sympathetic to her messages. Would-be cynics found her sincere in promoting her cause rather than in seeking notoriety for herself, placing her within appropriate feminine conventions. Willard never married, and although reporters regularly criticized other single reform leaders, such as Susan B. Anthony, as being spurned and bitter women, I have found no critical reference to Willard's marital status throughout the plethora of coverage she was given. Part of this probably derived from her charismatic personality, but it was also related to her fashioning the cause for women in acceptable terms. Willard claimed that temperance women were fighting for "home protection"; she foregrounded a daughter's devotion to parents, often speaking of her idyllic childhood and her love for her father and giving her mother a prominent place in all WCTU activities. She constantly reminded the public that she and other members of the WCTU were "womanly" women.

Reassuring New Places for Women

In addition to careful attention to their own dress and appearance, leaders of the WCTU recognized the rhetorical importance of the space associated with their public appearance. Just as women's characters and intent were closely associated with their bodily appearance, the spaces they used to conduct public meetings and to give speeches became significant as well. Based largely on beliefs about woman's place and need for protection, audiences and reporters carefully noted the appropriateness of meeting halls. Such notions had been prevalent throughout the second half of the century as women deliberately moved from their domestic sphere into increasingly public spaces. Anxiety with regard to space design in women's colleges is one testament to such concerns. Campus and building plans illustrated "the hopes and fears that accompanied the bold act of offering the higher learning to women" (Horowitz 3), with distinctive settings deemed appropriate for these new college students often allowing for "seclusion" and "enclosure" that reassured parents and critics. Similar apprehension accompanied women's move into nearly every unconventional space, from fears of their voting because polling places were often located in saloons, to concerns about their walking city streets unchaperoned.

Many women capitalized on such concerns, turning fears into reassurances. WCTU leaders prodded members to attend to details associated with meeting halls. For example, Caroline Buell suggested, "Make the place in which your meeting is to be held as attractive as possible" (28), and E. G. Greene insisted, "Remember to bring the flowers and mottoes, make the place cheery, giving forth a welcome" (48). Willard also regularly implored women to decorate with flowers and banners of their own work and design as well as with national flags and state escutcheons that contributed to the patriotic atmosphere. WCTU members hung the national motto and other temperance memorabilia throughout their meeting halls, almost always banners created by the handiwork of members. At nearly every convention, the women displayed needlework they had created themselves. For example, at the 1883 annual convention, Anna Gordon presented the Union with a banner she had embroidered herself, and the organization often honored select members by giving them quilts or other handmade articles created by local or state unions. Such examples of needlework allayed fears that these political women were not "true" women. Finally, members cloaked their conventions in patriotic fervor, displaying national flags and state shields at each meeting, even making special displays of patriotic acts. At the 1878 annual convention held in Baltimore, for example, they borrowed and displayed the national flag from Fort McHenry. Members always encouraged coverage that presented the reassuring feminine images they knew would dispel fear and criticism.

Predictable and similar descriptions of the decor of convention headquarters suggest that many newspapers also used descriptive information furnished by the WCTU when reporting on meetings. Often different newspapers in the same city gave nearly identical descriptions of the assembly halls in which the women were meeting. For example, when the national organization met in Chicago in 1877, the *Chicago Evening Journal* reported the meetings at Farwell Hall as follows:

> The stand and galleries of the hall have been elaborately decorated with flags and flowers. At the rear of the stage is the beautiful device or "coat of arms" of the National Temperance Union of Women. This was originated by Miss Frances E. Willard and Miss Mary A. Lathburg of New York. An immince [*sic*] cross of leaves and evergreens forms the center, around which are two large American flags and running vines. Above the cross is a star. Below is a century plant, indicative of the origin of the woman's movement so near the beginning of the new century, and beneath all is a beautiful monogram of the national society. The whole is surmounted with the motto, "For God and home and native land." ("Temperance Women" 4)

The *Inter-Ocean*'s description was similar:

> The rear of the stage, which attracted the attention of everyone, was beautifully decorated with the "coat of arms" of the association. The design was originated by Miss Frances E. Willard of this city, and Miss Mary A. Lathburg, of New York. The cross forms the center, on which lean the American flags. Below is the century plant, indicative of the origin of the woman's movement so near the beginning of the new century, and beneath all is a beautiful monogram of the society.

Above, in a graceful circle, is the motto in elegant letters, "For God and Home and Native Land." ("The Cause of the Crusades" 8)

Descriptive words, such as *beautiful*, and details specifying the significance of the century plant suggest prepared copy. Such detail was typical. When the organization met in Philadelphia, the *Philadelphia Inquirer* described the decor of the platform, noting that "a large basket of 500 flowers . . . came from Dover, Delaware, and was intended to represent the 500 members of the Temperance Union in that place" ("Modern Crusaders" 2), and in 1894, newspapers in Chicago noted the symbolism of the yellow and white decor—white representing the WCTU and yellow illustrating the National American Woman Suffrage Association ("White Ribbons Wave"; "Wine Is Their Foe").

Reporters are not likely to have perceived such symbolism in the decorations, and exact wording in more than one newspaper report outlined the "artistic and profuse" decorations. Major newspapers in almost every city elaborated on setting, speakers' backgrounds, and details of dress and appearance in a manner that suggests assistance from the WCTU Press Department. But reporters began to highlight "feminine" aspects of meeting halls for all women's organizations. When the National Woman Suffrage Association (NWSA) met in Indianapolis in May 1880, the *Indianapolis Journal,* which gave an "objective" report on resolutions, nominations, speeches, and proceedings in general, nonetheless described the halls precisely: "The stage of the Park Theater is appropriately and tastefully decorated with flags, flowers and plants. Hung around the proscenium boxes are mottoes expressive of the sentiments of the delegates" ("Woman Suffragists"). The only direct description that departed from factual relating of resolutions pertained to the hall dressing. Though the mottos hardly represented traditional "feminine" attitudes, displaying as they did such sayings as "Taxation without representation is tyranny," the atmosphere created by flowers, plants, and other accepted signs of femininity seemed designed to reassure reporters as well as make women comfortable.

Such attention to women's spaces was not relegated to conventions. When reporting the commemorative birthday celebration honoring Margaret Fuller, newspapers such as the *Boston Journal and Advertiser* and the *New York Tribune* devoted extensive coverage to "decorations," noting the "tasteful" use of "busts, portraits, and garlands of flowers" and describing in detail the "exquisite effect" of flower arrangements upon mantels and staircases, in chandeliers, and along windows ("Decorations" 182). Newspapers responded favorably to women's attention to presentation, both in bodily drapery and decor for meeting halls.

National Woman Suffrage Association

Leaders of other women's organizations exhibited concern for media coverage and stressed the importance of traditional dress for members as well. The most dramatic shift can be demonstrated by members of the suffrage associations.[2] From an earlier policy insistent on dress reform, leaders of the two major organizations assumed stances emphasizing that members should represent the organization in a manner of dignity. Having made the decision that the Bloomer costume had become a deterrent, whether to their own peace of mind or to the cause of woman's suffrage, they opposed any major deviation from traditional dress. In addition, the National Woman Suffrage Association obviously concerned itself with good coverage. Reporters mention, for example, Susan B. Anthony as "particularly accommodating to the reporters" ("Woman Suffragists").

The organizations' positions on dress are especially evident in their official newspapers. The NWSA's *Revolution* printed some articles on dress reform as well as letters from readers addressing the subject, but the official position for those representing the organization was that members should wear nothing that might impugn the movement. In fact, one highly visible member, Olive Logan, gave a series of speeches on dress in which she called for "reasonable" dress reform and lashed out at "indecent stagewomen." Logan, herself a former actress and regular contributor to the *Revolution,* received front-page coverage in the association's newspaper when she harshly reprimanded women who wore men's clothing. Based on her contention that "in every country among every people, the fashion is what constitutes the test of modesty or immodesty, of decency or indecency," Logan maintained that women who wore men's attire were "ridiculous, and that they take away from the strength of a cause which needs all the strength it can gain." To further emphasize her point, Logan celebrated those leaders who might "grace the salons of the most polished European court." She explained her pride in the leaders of her movement, whom she respected "far more for their graceful observance of womanly fashion in dress, than I could possibly have done if they had been sitting about me in ridiculous baggy trousers, in feeble imitation of the sex which is worthy imitation in better things" ("A Word").

Logan's charge purposefully differentiated leaders of the association from more radically attired women. To demonstrate the contrast, Logan described dignified and worthy representatives of the cause. Ironically, two of her examples had earlier worn and promoted the Bloomer dress, which was now seen as problematic:

Mrs. Stanton, beautifully attired in a trailing robe of black-and-gray silk, with a gay-colored silken scarf over her shapely shoulders, and her beautiful face aglow with sweetness all womanly. . . .

Mrs. Phelps, with superb gems at her neck and throat, elegant in black, richly trimmed, and Susan B. Anthony in a silk dress, plainer, but not less obedient to the laws of fashion. . . .

Anna Dickinson, with pearl-gray silk, trimmed with cherry satin; about her white throat a chain of gold to which was suspended a magnificent ornament composed of diamonds encircling a ruby fit for an Empress's crown, while over her shoulders hung a rich opera cloak—her pure face lovely with all that wins a woman's heart. ("A Word")

This emphasis on silk, satin, colors, and gemstones constitutes a remarkable shift from earlier insistence upon simple fabrics free of adornment; however, the colors reiterate the somber tints typical of reformers' wear during the earlier period. Both the jewelry and colors deliberately separated them from the showy and less expensive attire of lower-class women or those of questionable character. The costly wardrobes highlight the move of nearly all women speakers in the second half of the century to seek acceptance by demonstrating their "respectable" station in society, but, lest this be mistaken, Logan emphasized the women's "obedience" to the laws of fashion. No radicals these women.

Similarly, Stanton supported Logan's position:

No one feels the importance of a radical change in woman's dress more than we do. Yet we could neither wear nor recommend the costume called "the American dress," . . . once known as the "Bloomer dress," because though convenient, it is neither artistic nor attractive. ("More about Dress")

Stanton suggested that the sexes should "dress as nearly alike as possible," meaning in men's clothing, because of its convenience, so that women could be paid equally with men for similar work and as protection for young girls from the "outrages from brutal men." Unfortunately, Stanton claimed, "the law forbids woman thus to protect herself" (35), and opinions in the *Revolution* often protested against members who represented the organization in masculine clothing. Although Stanton's claim is understandable, since women were often detained for wearing men's dress, few statutes actually forbad women's wearing men's clothing. Stanton, daughter of a prominent lawyer and judge and brilliantly knowledgeable about statutes concerning women, surely knew the law in this regard. Most women so arrested were charged on counts of vagrancy, and if they could prove good standing, that is, establish their currency on expenses, they were released. In fact, George Francis Train,[3] the controversial figure whom Anthony and Stanton had supported in his bid for the presidency, had asked the staff of the *Revolution* to look into questions of such legality the previous year, but the editors never replied ("Letters from George Francis Train"). Stanton apparently found it rhetorically effective to attribute her change in mode of dress to men's laws while promoting acceptable dress for NWSA members.

Although the dress controversy received some coverage in their newspaper, leaders of the NWSA had obviously decided their energies were better placed elsewhere. When traveling on the lecture circuit, Stanton did speak to dress reform, but she spoke against restricting fashions that required young women to "pinch their waists, and cut off circulation of blood for a space of several inches around that part of the body" ("About Women"; "Mrs. Cady Stanton"). Stanton's demands for dress reform were no longer radical; they included acceptable complaints that might be found in nearly any journal available to the general public.

Later, the *Revolution* responded to the editor of the *Tribune,* who asked, "What is to be the costume of the emancipated woman?" The reply implicitly denigrates the issue of dress reform:

> We the strong-minded have been so busy with the real interest of women, which we are seeking first to understand, and then to labor for, that we have not had time to read up on all those "manuals of good society," and so must thus answer to our young friend:
>
> First, to thank him for the wide and deep interest he feels in all that pertains to us—gloves, chignons, yarn mittens, long trains, scarfs, and all the little nothings that go to make up a lady's toilet.
>
> Second, to remind him that we have always worn clothes, and that we wear them at other places besides conventions.
>
> Third . . . we have always advised women to dress as they chose, only regarding the health and ease of the body. ("Costume" 307)

Obviously unwilling to renew the controversy over dress reform that had embroiled them in years of anguish and, many believed, harmed their cause, leaders assumed a distance from such questions. Their inverse sarcasm and implied criticism that the locus of the editor's interest lay in incidentals such as chignons and yarn mittens, however, belie their sensitivity to and lack of distance from the subject. Having made a concerted effort to separate themselves from "radical" dress reform, they were obviously angry with this editor who tried to entangle them again in such controversy.

When women who wore men's clothing or who broke implicit sanctions against dress appeared at the national conventions, other members supported the censorship. After the 1869 Washington Suffrage Convention, for example, NWSA member Grace Greenwood, a Washington correspondent for the *New York Times,* reprimanded Dr. Mary Walker. After praising the more traditionally dressed, such as the "Quaker gentlewoman, Lucretia Mott," Greenwood wrote,

> I think some authority there should be to exclude or silence persons unfit to appear before an intelligent and refined audience—some power to rule out utterly, and keep out, ignorant or insane men and women who realize some of the worst things falsely charged against the leaders of this movement.
>
> I allude to certain anomalous creatures, in fearful hybrid costumes, who, a-thirst for distinction, and not possessing the brain, culture, or moral force to acquire it, content themselves with a vulgar notoriety, gained by the defiance of social laws, proprieties, and decencies, by measureless assumption and vanity, and by idiotic eccentricity of dress. (66)

Greenwood's comments were reported in the *Revolution,* to which she was a regular contributor. Her portrayal of an "intelligent and refined" audience depicts members as public figures of "taste" who disdain the radical. While the editors of the *Revolution* did not comment explicitly on her position, their presentation of her as a celebrity condoned her criticism of any who dressed differently.[4]

American Woman Suffrage Association

The other large wing of the suffrage movement, the American Woman Suffrage Association (AWSA), rarely insisted openly that members adhere to accepted standards of dress; however, concern for the rhetorical impact of dress is clear. Many AWSA members, including Mary Livermore and Julia Ward Howe, were also active in the WCTU. AWSA members' exposure to and complicity in the philosophies of the WCTU suggest their alignment on such issues.

Newspaper reports of annual meetings demonstrate that members dressed carefully for their public appearances and that their impact was effective. For example, in announcing the AWSA's coming meeting in Louisville in 1881, the first time the association had met so far south, the *Courier Journal* expressed wonder at the convention's being held so far out of the way, taking it as evidence that the people of other cities had grown tired of the subject ("Woman Suffrage" 1881). Immediately prior to the convention, the *Courier Journal* insisted that

> this last twenty years have convinced the women of this generation that they do not want to vote; that it would be harmful to the country and themselves if they could vote, and that of all the trouble and grievances, real or imaginary, under which they suffer, the denial of the elective franchise is the most far-fetched and imaginary of them all. ("The Woman Suffrage Movement")

After the convention had convened, however, the *Courier Journal*'s reportage typifies the approval expressed by those covering women's conventions when, expecting to see outrageously dressed women, they encountered what they deemed to be refined and proper ladies. Dress denoting cultivated middle-class women assuaged reporters' concern about the women's characters, and the reporters then offered assurances to readers. After informing readers that "ninety per cent of them are married ladies" and that their dress was that of "ladies," the reporter acknowledged the "wildly extravagant . . . general conception" of woman's suffrage conventions: "The impression, indeed, seems to have been general that an advocate of woman's rights must of necessity wear her hair short, and sport pantaloons cut after the most approved fashion of the male person."

Noting the "handsomely dressed" and "thoroughly womanly ladies" present at the convention, the report continued by describing "two or three of the toilets" for the purpose of assuring the public "that there is nothing uncouth in the dress or appearance of the woman's rights advocates:

> Mrs. Helen Gougar, the editor of *Our Herald* . . . wore an elegant Parisian walking dress of maroon velvet and satin de Lyon, with point lace collar, white linen cuffs, and handsome gold ornaments.
> Mrs. J. P. Fuller, a magnificent-looking brunette, of St. Louis, Mo., was attired in an elegantly fitting street dress of black brocaded satin trimmed with beads of passementerie; diamond ornaments. . . .
> Miss Mary F. Eastman, of Boston, was tastefully attired in a heavy black silk walking suit, with diamond ornaments. ("The Suffragists" 2)

A notable feature here is the meticulous attention to detail atypical of reporters. The *Courier Journal* surely received prepared copy, evidenced by the specific and intricate attention to such features as types of satins and laces. The description of expensive clothing and jewels attests to both the class bias involved in acceptance of public women and the degree to which dress and appearance shaped notions of class. During the latter part of the century, approval of women speakers correlated highly with proper clothing and appropriate appearance. The description in the *Courier Journal* ended by noting that "most of the other ladies wore walking suits of black silk, the fact being noticeable that there was not a single cloudy costume among them" ("The Suffragists" 2), an encouraging sign for those fearful of major ruptures in the traditional societal structure.

The AWSA's official newspaper, *Woman's Journal,* treated dress reform as a far more important subject than did the *Revolution.* Throughout its history, in nearly every issue, the *Journal* printed letters and articles advocating dress reform. It reported regularly on meetings of the American Free Dress League and the National Dress Reform Association. One major discussion in the *Woman's Journal* during the 1870s concerned a proper and more positive name for the American dress, or reformed dress. Various names, such as the chemijugie, the chemette, and the chemile gained support, and readers and editors continued to insist upon the necessity for reform. However, at meetings where members represented the organization visibly and publicly, they carefully projected an ethos that reassured newspaper reporters and editors as well as their readers.

Black Women's Organizations

The organizations discussed to this point were made up primarily of white women. If white women speakers felt the need to carefully address ethical appearance, concern for dress and appearance among African American women speakers, though necessarily more complicated, was equally acute. Toward the end of the century, as Paula Giddings has demonstrated, "One of the first items of business of the Black leaders' agenda was to defend their moral integrity as women" (85). In fact, charges against the morality of black women were a major impetus in the formation of black women's clubs near the end of the century, inspiring Josephine St. Pierre Ruffin's call for black women leaders to "stand before the world and declare ourselves and our principles" (qtd. in S. Logan, *With Pen* 120). Ruffin's incensed call was in response to the specific charge of John W. Jacks, president of the Missouri Press Association, who claimed that black women were "wholly devoid of morality and that they were prostitutes, thieves and liars" (120). While Jacks's accusation provided a precise focus for Ruffin, notions behind his claims had been prevalent for some time. Cast as immoral and inferior, black women "felt they had a compelling mandate" (Giddings 83) to dispel prejudicial and negative images about black women. One measure of such attainment was the exemplification of the "lady," and dress was intrinsically intertwined with that notion. To establish positive images, black women speakers generally dressed modestly and usually after the fashion assumed by white middle-class women. They hesitated to draw attention specifically to their bodies. Carla Peterson suggests that descriptions of Harper's delivery as quiet, with feminine modesty, represent an "attempt to eliminate the public presence of the black female body perceived as sexualized or grotesque and to promote the voice as pure melody, insubstantial sound, a negation of presence" (124). Harper was the most visible of black women in primarily white women's organizations; however, other African American women were acutely aware of the social context in which they spoke as well.

The *Woman's Era,* the newspaper of the black women's clubs, contains little discussion of dress, either the reform dress or other attire that might be considered appropriate, and the focus for this newspaper differed from such newspapers as the *Revolution* and the *Woman's Journal.* Both the black women's clubs and the newspaper itself were younger than the white women's organizations and newspapers and had a different purpose. Black women placed much rhetorical value on dress, however. That concern is perhaps best demonstrated in Ida B. Wells's account of her wedding. Pleased that the *New York Age,* a leading black-owned newspaper, was "largely copied in the Negro papers throughout the country" (Wells 239), Wells includes the copy in her autobiography, detailing the dress of participants much as white-owned newspapers would for middle- and upper-class white women, noting the bridesmaids dressed in "lemon crepe, white ribbons, slippers and white gloves," and the bride "dressed in white satin en train, trimmed with chiffon and orange blossoms" (239–40). Of even greater significance, Wells is flattered that the Women's Republican State Central Committee attended the ceremony "dressed in honor of the occasion in evening attire, just the same as if they had attended a wedding among themselves. This we considered a very great honor" (241). Supremely aware of the significance of dress, Wells prized the message delivered by notable attendees in attire retained for the most special occasions. For her, the rhetorical performance of the committee's wearing of formal attire—their dressing for her occasion just as they would for significant whites—performed the ultimate rhetorical act signifying her importance.

Middle-class women throughout the second half of the century were identified largely according to appearance, and black middle-class women's attention to dress and manner, they hoped, would provide a measure of safety for them. Often that was true. Well-to-do blacks, such as Mary Ann Shadd (Cary) and Sarah Remond, for example, moved freely and with respect within their hometowns where their families were recognized and well regarded. When they left the environs that afforded them such recognition, however, they, too, often faced derogation based on race. Even their usual habitats did not always ensure respect for black women. Thus, the San Francisco black-owned newspaper, *Pacific Appeal,* complained when "inferiors" ignored dress as a determinant of value: "We often hear of gross insults being offered to respectable and well dressed colored ladies by the conductors of the horse railroad cars" (qtd. in Yee 134). In the nineteenth century, when class determined degree of respect and dress so clearly defined class, well-to-do African Americans expected treatment superior to that ordinarily given to the poor. However, regardless of wealth, dress spoke differently for black women because whites usually attended to complexion before dress. In addition, their purposes differed somewhat from those of white women. While white women were *reclaiming* an ethos, that of the "lady," black women were trying to *attain* that ethos.

Another difference in response was exhibited in the lack of attention that the press paid the gatherings of black women. Ida B. Wells complained that the white press was "dumb" when it came to concerns of blacks (86). In fact, many of what we now consider very important meetings of black women were not recognized in contemporary white-owned newspapers, and in those where they were reported, rarely did accounts of black women's meetings include the details of dress that served as markers of character for white women. Black women speakers were most often recognized in white-owned newspapers when they appeared as part of white women's organizations, such as the national meetings of the WCTU. Throughout the second half of the century when black women appeared publicly and were acknowledged, however, they were typically identified by skin color and by dress only if it differed from that traditionally worn by white women.

Dress had become a means of praising and accepting white women speakers; however, reporters pointed to the otherness of black women speakers by noting skin color and ignoring dress. Perhaps they hesitated to describe features that identified them with white middle-class women, as they dressed similarly in conventionally tasteful clothing. For example, newspaper reports, both in headings and in leads, either noted the appearance of "a young colored woman" or made reference to her color parenthetically: "Mrs. Thurman (colored) presented . . ." Thus, Thurman wore both the Mrs., sign of her sex and marital status, and (colored) mark of her race, but no other item of identification.[5] This was typical throughout the second half of the century. Even the editors of the *History of Woman Suffrage,* who carefully praise such black leaders as Sojourner Truth and Frederick Douglass, often made color the defining feature of identity. For example, when presented in the *History,* Frances Harper is so identified: introduced as part of the conversation, the editors present her to readers as "Mrs. Harper (colored)" (1: 391). When Sojourner Truth appeared at New York's Metropolitan Hall as part of the New York City Anti-Slavery Society, the *New York Daily Tribune* introduced her speech by noting, "Mrs. Sojourner Truth, an old colored woman" ("Mrs. Sojourner Truth" 5).[6]

Sojourner Truth

Women whose appearances were exceptional, such as Sojourner Truth, often found themselves described beyond color, but such presentation demonstrates the need to dress black women differently rather than to provide coverage similar to that given white women. Truth apparently used her body and dress to confound surly critics who denied her the common courtesy extended to "ladies." When Dr. T. W. Strain questioned her sex, insisting that the women present check for breasts to prove that she was not a man disguised in woman's dress, Truth exposed her breasts to silence him (Sterling 151). But generally Truth enveloped her black body in dress representing white middle-class standards. Her only "African" vestige of dress was the turban she wore at all public appearances, a piece of apparel that would also conceal the textured hair that distanced her from features identified with a lady. The ideal of femininity rested on white middle-class values that prized silky straight or wavy hair.

Frances Gage's famous reminiscence of Truth's presentation at the 1853 Woman's Rights Convention in Akron, Ohio, highlights both Truth's color and clothing: "The leaders of the movement trembled on seeing a tall, gaunt black woman in a gray dress and white turban, surmounted with an uncouth sun-bonnet, march deliberately into the church" (Stanton et al. 115)—Gage's use of such words as *gaunt* and *uncouth* are hardly representative of contemporary standards of taste. Truth, according to Gage, "stood nearly six feet high" (116). Her large frame and unique figure drew comments from both women's and men's newspapers. When she spoke at the New York Unitarian Church, even the *Revolution,* which usually avoided identifying women by appearance, remarked on Truth's "tall and vigorous frame," and then described her further:

> Her very appearance is remarkable. . . . Her face carries out the strength suggested by her figure. Her pure African color, deep black, is toned down by no perceptible tinge of Caucasian blood; on her head she wears a large white turban, which entirely conceals any natural covering which may have been left to her; and a pair of large spectacles add to the novelty of her appearance. ("Sojourner Truth" 44)

Perhaps most typical here is the reference to Truth's "pure African color, deep black." Caucasians' concern with pure blood often led to their identifying speakers according to shades of color. Nell Irvin Painter suggests that the "apparent lack of white ancestry, which would have offered a facile explanation for her intelligence" (256), fascinated a white culture. Harriet Beecher Stowe remembered Truth in terms of color and appearance as well: "She was evidently a full-blooded African. . . . Her tall form is still vivid to my mind. She was dressed in some stout, grayish stuff, neat and clean, though dusty from travel. On her head she wore a bright Madras handkerchief arranged as a turban" ("Sojourner Truth" 473).

Truth, of course, was aware of the otherness she presented and of its potential rhetorical power. According to those who reported her appearances, she repeatedly demonstrated her acute sense of presence and humored whites who wished to inscribe their notions of blackness onto her body. When introduced at the Akron convention, Truth "moved slowly and solemnly to the front, laid her bonnet at her feet, and turned her great speaking eyes" to Gage. With her "uncouth bonnet," Truth effectively held her audience's attention, directing their eyes, timing her first words at her will and according to her own immaculate sense of presentation. Her large frame, which placed her outside conventional expectations of femininity, also became an effective rhetorical device for her according to reporters. "Look at my arm!" she insisted, baring her arm to demonstrate the powerful muscles she had developed as a slave (Stanton et al. 116). If descriptions of her presentations are accurate, Truth often used her body as an explicit representation of the history of slavery in this country. Her scars became the dress/text that she wished her audience to read, her platform resembling the auction block upon which so many Africans had been sold. Stowe notes Truth's "stretching her scarred hands towards the glory to be revealed," a particularly compelling comment on the vestiges of her slave experience (477), and Frances Titus similarly notes Truth's use of corporeal evidence at a speech during the Civil War: "She undid the collar of her dress and bared her arms, to the shoulders, showing them covered with a perfect network of scars made by the slave master's lash" (qtd. in Fitch 430).

Nearly all of the readings of Truth's use of body are retrospective. Late-twentieth-century historians, most recently Painter, convincingly contend that the retrospective descriptions of Truth are more fiction than fact; they demonstrate in the recorders' focus, nonetheless, the rhetorical power of the black woman's body and its intimate connection with ethical presentation. I would suggest, as well, that the overwhelming authoritative ethos presented in the text of Truth's body was based to some degree on actuality. It seems inconceivable that the many stories of her outstanding rhetorical impact could be entirely fictional. More likely, her presence was described in terms more readily expressible by a white audience. Truth was conscious of the correlation between her dress and appearance and her acceptance as a "lady." Most descriptions suggest a generally subdued clothing characteristic of the various religious communities to which she belonged. And most photographs of Truth demonstrate her "expertly tailored clothing made of handsome, substantial material" (Painter 187), a simple yet tasteful quality in her dress that would have aligned her with both religious and ladylike qualities. In noting the selling of her photographs for charitable purposes, Painter claims, "In none of these portraits is there anything beyond blackness that would inspire charity—nothing of the piteous slave mother . . . no bared arms, no bodice taken down in public"; showing "a solid bourgeoise . . . with only her face and hands uncovered, hers is the antithesis of a naked body" (196). This bourgeois, "proper" presentation is the very ethical presentation that permitted Truth to become an acceptable speaker among white audiences. Welcomed in the homes of leading reformers and celebrities, joining them at receptions and on platforms, Truth provided the complexion upon which a cause might be hung, all the while presenting the appropriate dress and manner that comforted reformers and newspaper reporters alike.

One instance that demonstrates whites' need to dress Truth "appropriately" also illustrates the powerful rhetorical impact of clothing. In Steuben County, Indiana, women of the National Woman's Loyal League invited Truth to participate in antislavery rallies:

> The ladies thought I should be dressed in uniform, so they put upon me a red, white, and blue shawl, a sash and apron to match a cap on my head with a star in front, and a star on each shoulder. When I was dressed I looked in the glass and was fairly frightened. (qtd. in Sterling 251)

Truth likely did look ridiculous in such clothing. The attempts of these white women to dress Truth in patriotic attire, even as they played the "Star-Spangled Banner," may attest to their need to dress an "African" as an "American" in order to signify her patriotism by conventional standards. But the covering of Truth/truth by a patriotic ardor might also represent a "ladylike" effort at denying or glossing over a troublesome subtext at a national celebration. The costume, nonetheless, angered those who found a black woman's representation of America offensive. Although Truth had spoken in Indiana numerous times, on this occasion she was arrested.

Truth sometimes disturbed suffrage leaders by criticizing members who, she claimed, pandered to current fashion. Commenting on the 1870 American Woman Suffrage Association convention, Truth reprimanded women she felt dressed inappropriately for reformers:

> I'm awful hard on dress, you know. Women, you forget that you are the mothers of creation; you forget your sons were cut off like grass by the war, and the land was covered with their blood; you rig yourselves up in panniers and Grecian bend-backs and flummeries; yes, and mothers and gray haired grandmothers wear high-heeled shoes and humps on their heads, and put them on their babies, and stuff them out so that they keel over when the wind blows. Oh mothers, I'm ashamed of ye! When I saw them women on the stage at the Woman Suffrage Convention, the other day, I thought, what kind of reformers be you, with goose wings on your heads, as if you were going to fly, and dressed in such ridiculous fashion, talking about reform and women's rights? 'Pears to me you had better reform yourselves first. But Sojourner is an old body and will soon go out of this world into another, and wants to say when she gets there, "Lord, I have done my duty, I have told the whole truth, and kept nothing back." ("'Sojourner Truth' on the Fashions" 356)

Unlike Stanton and others who were speaking in favor of dress reform but distanced the organization from anything but moderate change, Truth identified the unseemly or inappropriate dress with members of the organization, making others' general criticism specific and angering suffrage leaders.

Editors of the *Woman's Journal* retorted that the "style of dress on the platform on that occasion [was] unusually plain and simple" (356). Denying the presence of panniers and Grecian bends, they noted the "everlasting to everlasting" complaint of women's dress. Evidence of the sensitivity surrounding this subject surfaces in the editors' response:

> While we would not think of criticizing Sojourner's style of dress, we cannot help thinking that if "these reformers" should follow the fashion which she sets in her own person, they would be as extreme, and as ridiculous in appearance, as are the most consecrated devotees of the present ridiculous fashions. Considerations of beauty, grace and taste in dress do not seem to us unworthy a woman—a true woman, or a woman "reformer," and we should condemn the angularities, the ungracefulness and the absolute deformity of a dress like Sojourner Truth's, as severely as she would "panniers," "Grecian bend-backs," etc. (356)

Few reformers criticized one another's dress except when it was seen to bring disparaging comments because of its deviance from femininity, as in the case of masculine dress. Probably few women at the convention actually wore the nouveau styles Truth mentions, but her drawing attention to those who did broke an unspoken rule among members of the organization.

Members dressed in a fashion that would find approval for the cause, and they demonstrated concern only for those who dressed in a manner that offended current taste. Having claimed a middle ground between the radical and the frivolous, leaders were rankled by hints that members were pandering to the petty fads of fashion with elaborate panniers. Truth risked a return to earlier days of focused criticism on reform women's dress, but the vitriol with which leaders attacked her "ungracefulness" and "absolute deformity" of dress is surprising. The response demonstrates the sensitivity to criticism about their dress among suffrage leaders who so carefully worked to present an appropriate appearance. While leaders might "not think of criticizing Sojourner's style of dress," when given what they deemed a fair opportunity they blithely noted any features of her dress that deviated from expected norms of taste for white middle-class women.

Frances E. W. Harper

Identification of black women speakers by color continued throughout the century. When the eloquent and highly respected Frances Ellen Watkins Harper spoke, she was generally identified by color. Indeed, her complexion seems to have been the only significant factor for some reporters. When she spoke in Newark at the 1876 national WCTU convention, the *Newark Daily Advertiser* recognized her as "Mrs. Francis Hopper, a colored lady from Philadelphia" ("WCTU" 2), and although Grace Greenwood's description of Harper notes her "noble head" and intends to praise by naming her a "bronze muse," her description is, nonetheless, particularized according to color (Sterling 160). So went attention to Harper throughout the century. After a lecture in Maine, the *Portland Advertiser* reported that "Miss W. is slightly tinged with African blood, but the color only serves to add a charm to the occasion which nothing else could give" (Sterling 161).

Like Truth, Harper sometimes focused attention on her own dress to make a statement:

> I have reason to be thankful that I am able to give a little more for a Free Labor dress, if it is coarser. I can thank God that upon its warp and woof I see no stain of blood and tears; that to procure a little finer muslin for my limbs no crushed and broken heart went out in sighs. (qtd. in Sterling 160)

As did Truth, Harper called attention to her body only to create a textured fabric of her history as a black woman and its relationship to American slavery. In representing her people, she carefully made a statement about the evils of slavery, symbolically weaving the crushing reality of slavery with the weave of her own dress.

Positioning Black Women as "True Women"

The number of black women speakers increased dramatically as the nineteenth century drew to a close. Angered by unfair stereotypical perceptions, black women responded to Ruffin's call to organize. Ruffin had stated as one purpose "to teach an ignorant and suspicious world that our aims and interests are identical with those of all good aspiring women" (Davis 18). Accordingly, speakers generally wore clothing that situated them within nineteenth-century Christian notions of the lady. Beverly Guy-Sheftall notes that Gertrude Bustill Mossell's best-known book, *The Work of the Afro-American Woman,* was written "to affirm the noble womanhood of black women who were excluded from racist and classist concepts of 'true women'" (55). Mossell's first column for T. Thomas Fortune's New York *Freeman* promised to "promote true womanhood, especially that of the African race" (qtd. in Guy-Sheftall 55). Similarly, in her speech "The Progress of Colored Women," Mary Church Terrell notes the surprise of white women at the "intelligence, culture, and taste in dress which the colored women displayed" (qtd. in Guy-Sheftall 64). An ability to present the marks of acceptable middle-class standards was a measure of progress for African American women among both blacks and whites.

Occasionally black women speakers drew attention to their persons in order to accentuate this similarity, especially when speaking before white audiences. In "The Awakening of the Afro-American Woman," delivered before the annual convention of the Society of Christian Endeavor in 1897, a primarily white audience, Victoria Earl Matthews highlighted black women's connection with white women in such a manner: "As I stand here to-day in the garments of Christian womanhood, the horrible days of slavery, out of which I came, seem as a dream that is told, some horror incredible" (qtd. in S. Logan, *With Pen* 150). Matthews denoted the progress black women had made specifically by demonstrating her Christian persona with a metaphorical reference that would have highlighted her own appropriate and acceptable dress.

Still, as the end of the century neared, black women speakers continued to be underrepresented and misrepresented by newspapers. When the Congress of Representative Women met in Chicago in 1893, newspapers gave elaborate front-page coverage to the meeting, including illustrations (see fig. 5.2), often printing speeches as well. Black women who belonged to major organizations occasionally received a mention in the coverage, even if incorrect. For example, the *Chicago Daily Tribune* did report that Francis [Frances] Harper and Hattie O. [Hallie Q.] Brown, "leaders among colored women," were present at the Congress. The *Chicago Herald* marveled over the variety of women speakers, "from the Countess of Aberdeen to the former slave, Francis E. W. Harper, of Philadelphia" ("Woman's Congress"); on another occasion the newspaper reported part of Harper's speech but headed that portion with "Daughter of a Slave Speaks." Contrary to reports in the *Herald,* Harper was born free to free parents, and the use of the

Fig. 5.2. The Congress of Women, *Chicago Times,* 16 May 1893.

masculine spelling of her name recalls charges of masculinity leveled at earlier speakers. Numerous full-length and partial illustrations of many of the women speakers were included in reports. None of the black women were included.

Finally, in the 1890s, black women, it appears, were deemed of enough importance for newspapers to present visual descriptions, either in print or graphics. In 1894, at least two depictions of black women speakers suggest recognition of their significance. When Ida B. Wells appeared in New York in her effort to expose the realities of lynching in the South, the New York *Sun* announced "the young colored woman who has been telling the English people about the outrages which her race is subjected to in the South" followed by a description of her dress: "Miss Wells wore a plain black dress and a white Leghorn hat, ornamented with long white ostrich feathers" ("Ida Wells Heard Here" 2). And the *New York Tribune* similarly announced "the young colored woman" with a description of her person: "She is apparently about twenty-four years old, of medium height, and has a light complexion" ("She Pleads for Her Race" 7). Wells had gained enough celebrity that newspapers felt a need to provide readers with details of her appearance. The coverage, of course, furthered her celebrity as well.

The following year, when the WCTU held its annual national meeting in Baltimore, the *Baltimore Herald* presented full body sketches of the most important leaders of the convention. Along with white leaders, the newspaper included a full-length illustration of Frances Harper (see fig. 5.3). The portrayal, equally specific in detail to that of other leaders, shows a dignified Harper, dressed simply but tastefully. Even black women's organizations began to receive attention. The *Chicago Tribune* reported the meeting of the National Association of Colored Women's Clubs held in Chicago in 1899 with portraits of the three women elected to offices (see fig. 5.4). The upper body depictions demonstrate women dressed and groomed as "ladies" would be expected to dress. Taken together the coverage of these black women leaders at the end of the century demonstrates a greater acceptance of black women speakers.

Although we may be uncomfortable with the focus on women's bodies and dress today, at the turn of the nineteenth century such concern contributed to women speakers' success, signifying their importance and acceptability. Women speakers unquestionably recognized such support and dressed in a manner that furthered a positive ethos. Dress had become a defining feature, often promoting celebrity and providing a measure by which audiences might be reassured that if women were claiming a new place, they at least maintained their appropriate "feminine" and class stations.

Fig. 5.3. Frances Ellen Watkins Harper, sketch from *Baltimore Morning Herald*, 20 October 1895.

NEW OFFICERS CHOSEN AT THE COLORED WOMEN'S CONVENTION.

MRS. JOSEPHINE B. BRUCE.
First Vice President.

MRS. LUCY PHILLIPS.
Second Vice President.

MRS. MARY CHURCH TERRELL.
President.

Fig. 5.4. Newly elected officers, National Association of Colored Women's Clubs, *Chicago Tribune*, 17 August 1899.

Conclusion: Dress and Body as Spectacle

Take off the robes, and put on the pants, and show the limbs, and grace and mystery is all gone.
> —Reverend John Todd, qtd. in Woodward

She beguiles and blinds men by her smiles and her bland and winning voice.
> —Henry G. Ludlow, *Liberator*

*T*his project began with my search for new ways to write women into the history of rhetoric. Sensing that women have been made invisible partly because we have misinterpreted their very high visibility, I focused my examination on the body and appearance as crucial to understanding women's participation in public forums. The place of the gendered body has historically been peripheral to the study of rhetoric, primarily because rhetoric has been seen in terms of men, and masculine constructs of the body have been synonymous with oratory. Elizabeth Grosz's suggestion that the body has been "a conceptual blind spot in both mainstream Western philosophical thought and contemporary feminist theory" (3) is particularly true in the study of rhetoric. In addressing women's significance we have paid surprisingly little attention to the body, perhaps the greatest barrier women speakers faced due to the cultural and material reality of their bodies.

The rhetorical tradition has included some study of posture and gestures, but the focus has been on the masculine body. In the eighteenth and nineteenth centuries, for example, rhetorical exercises focused much attention on bodily positioning and movement. Yet such study has been all but useless in understanding women's rhetoric, as women either could not or dared not make use of such suggestions. Even had they attempted to use the traditional movements deemed appropriate for men, their dress would have restricted that movement. In her popular book on dress for women, *What to Wear,* nineteenth-century novelist and dress reformer Elizabeth Stuart Phelps includes the narrative of a professor of elocution who taught "both sexes":

> When I first gave lessons at the Young Ladies' Seminaries, I was greatly puzzled. Some of my exercises are calisthenic, and require active movements of the arms. To my surprise, the girls could not meet their hands above their heads; many of them could not raise them half way to the required point. I was a young man, and did not know much about a lady's dress; and for some time the reason of this did not occur to me. At length I bethought me, that their mode of dress was at fault. I have been obliged to discontinue entirely the use of those exercises in girls' schools, though I think them very important to the elocutionist. (66)

While dress itself created physical restrictions for women, the fracture of expected images would likely have alarmed audiences. Cultural convention held large, expansive movements to be masculine. In order to be feminine, women moved fluidly, with small movements close to the body. Theirs was a different situation from that for men, inscribed with specific visual expectations not conducive to traditional public presentation. The construction of the decorated woman with tiny, restricted movements contributed to a visual pleasure firmly ensconced in nineteenth-century culture that worked against oratorical authority.

The elaborately adorned nineteenth-century pedestaled woman invoked spectatorial images that inevitably influenced and affected women public speakers. Scholars have associated scopophilic interest most closely with twentieth-century displays, especially with regards to film. However, the spectatorial nature of nineteenth-century culture is evident in the excitement over dioramas, kaleidoscopes, and panopticons as well as in the extensive emphasis on women's dress. Periodicals with elaborate steel engravings featured the ostentatiously dressed woman as the primary interest. The effect continued in broadsides and advertisements for music, theater, and other forms of entertainment. Reports of many nineteenth-century events can easily be read as tableaux, so that the reader can imagine scenes decorated with ornamented and lavishly dressed women.

Women—at least the ideal women presented in periodicals, newspapers, and literature by midcentury—dressed in clothing that accentuated the body, from the corseted hourglass shapes to the revealing necklines that highlighted the breast. The classed nature of the culture surrounding the ideal woman supported notions of her unattainableness and, therefore, her greater desirability; however, that desire was eclipsed by men's widely voiced concerns for sheltering and protecting women. Notions of women's purity and lack of sexual passion also averted attention from desire for the decorative woman. Cultural conventions collaborated in perpetuating the myth of women as private and chaste in spite of the fact that they were so often on display. Protected, chaste, middle-class women represented the private possessions of fathers and then husbands—desirable and unattainable.

The epigraphs that begin this conclusion demonstrate the simultaneity of fears created at the intersection of this spectatorial image and the public platform. When women began to rebel against the ornamented clothing of desire—when they adopted clothing less complicit in the silence and "look" of the desirable and unattainable woman—fear of lost scopophilic pleasure surfaced repeatedly in hysterical reactions to the dress. Although dress reformers repeatedly asserted their intention to change women's dress in a variety of ways—shortening skirts, eliminating tight lacing and corsetting, reducing the need for voluminous petticoats and crinolines, and covering more fully the exposed upper areas of the body—critics insisted that women's primary concern was with dress length and that shortening clothing slightly would adequately provide the changes women needed. Even those men offering support for the reform insisted that shortening skirts to eliminate their dragging along dirty floors would suffice. This barely abbreviated skirt failed to eliminate the coveted image of women as constructed by nineteenth-century culture, leaving in place the aura of the fragile, protected, unattainable woman.

Women's Power

This sense of loss to women's "look" was complemented by fear of their power as they began leaving the "sheltered" place that framed the myth of their pedestaled existence. Moving from the parlor where they provided a constant and safe specimen for view, some chose the platform, a location no longer passive and controlled for private scopic pleasure, no longer captured as in a steel fashion plate to be viewed on demand; these women no longer averted their eyes in the demure fashion demanded by nineteenth-century conventions.

In order to understand the fear associated with this active look of women speakers, it is helpful to examine the depth of convention that forbade women to return men's look directly. Women were expected to pretend that they were not being watched. Even when approached directly, custom demanded that they keep eyes lowered. Assuming the privilege of looking directly at another undermined the power structure that helped to keep gendered and classed hierarchies in place. The lower classes, especially slaves and free blacks, and women were expected to make eye contact only with others of their station, not with their superiors. The strength of these customs was even more apparent in oratory. The most frequent cry against women speakers initially was not related to their speech but to their addressing "promiscuous" audiences. That women could usurp the power of looking directly at (and often down upon) men was shocking. As the Grimkés toured New England, irate ministers and newspaper editors said little as long as the sisters confined their addresses to other women. They became incensed, however, at the idea of women's addressing audiences that included men.

Even in progressive educational institutions, such as Oberlin College, women were denied participation in men's rhetoric classes, although they were eventually permitted attendance only. By 1858, concessions were made allowing women to read their compositions at graduation, but the rationale behind the reading was that women thus kept eyes lowered rather than directly addressing the audience. As late as 1870, Harriet Keeler shocked her Oberlin graduation audience by declining to read her composition demurely with eyes lowered but instead looking directly at her audiences while she spoke (Lawrence 78–80).

As Frederic Jameson has noted, the gaze represents a blatant power relation, restricting to the privileged the "right to look" (7). Changing the dynamics of the gaze, diminishing the carefully controlled privilege that restricts the right to satisfy curiosity, to experience pleasure, necessarily alters power structures. Women's moving to the platform unveiled the spectatorial and voyeuristic reality of women's place. The gaze was altered and exposed, diminishing the pleasure of the spectacle and invoking the fear so commonly expressed in periodicals. Seen from a psychoanalytic perspective, the extraordinary and seemingly irrational fear may be readily connected to references to the supernatural and monstrous. Ludlow's reference evokes the Medusa myth best, but others suggest similar fears. Women speakers were called Amazons, brazen creatures, strange specimens of humanity, and mistakes of nature. Their power was referred to in terms of witchcraft and magic or, as in the case of Amazons, size. Terms of criticism referred more often to the power of sight than to hearing. That a woman speaker might blind men, as Henry Ludlow suggested, attests to her compelling power of representation.

The Symbolic Power of Dress

Dress is equally complicit in power arrangements as evidenced by the many instances of the powerless appropriating the dress of the more powerful. Although men were occasionally arrested for wearing women's clothing, such happenings were rare, and rather than expressing fear in those situations, authorities appeared to be disgusted that a man would assume the garments of the less powerful and less worthy. The rhetoric concerning men's and women's dress reflected such assumptions. In expressing concern for women's "borrowed feathers," the *Saturday Evening Post* suggested the desire behind women's traditional dress: "By a proper concealment of form, it also tends to increase that mystery which is never found separated from the highest feelings of our nature." But the newspaper also demonstrated the implicit power relation seen in men's and women's dress: "If they rightfully belong to him, they cannot belong to her; and if they belong to her, they cannot, without shame, be worn by him" ("The Great Trouser Movement"). Men assumed a right to sole proprietorship of masculine clothing, suggesting its value, but attached disgrace to men who would condescend to wear women's dress.

Similarly, slaves might assume dress for crossing gender boundaries, even from masculine to feminine, but temporarily for extraordinary reasons. Servants and slaves more likely dressed in imitation of their employers and owners, with the governing classes expressing both concern and fear at such appropriation. When not considered dangerous, dressing out of station, that is, men assuming women's clothing and whites taking on blacks' appearance, provided for amusement. In *Uncle Tom's Cabin,* Adolph's wearing Augustine St. Clare's clothing provides humor because of Adolph's pretensions to a higher station, but Huck Finn's donning a girl's garments provides a greater opportunity for comic pleasure because the reversal in power relations is more preposterous. Adolph may wish he could occupy St. Clare's position, but Huck's cross-dressing is understood as a temporary, pragmatic effort to gain information. He would never choose such a role permanently. The incident provides a memorable, comic episode because of its singularity.

The extremely popular minstrel performances were fraught with complicated notions about race and gender in the nineteenth century, but, as with Huck Finn, much of the humor was derived from the ridiculousness of the more powerful taking on the appearance of the weak. Men dressed as "wenches" with whites masquerading as blacks. In 1841, editor Thomas Law Nichols explained P. T. Barnum's consternation at losing his most popular and profitable minstrel dancer, John Diamond. In his efforts to replace Diamond, Barnum discovered an individual who could "dance a better break-down than Master Diamond." The problem, though, was that the replacement was black, and according to Nichols, "There was not an audience in America that would not have resented, in a very energetic fashion, the insult of being asked to look at the dancing of a real negro" (qtd. in Lott 112). Despite complex implications of racial issues here, a major problem for Barnum was that a black man performing as a black man would have greatly lessened the ridiculous and therefore the comic pleasure of the performance.

"'Acting the wench' was wildly popular" in minstrel acts as well (Lott 164). Lillian Schlissel suggests that "genital guessing" in "wench" performances did not "diffuse sexuality"; instead, the "game of sexual identity took on new intensity when the players were 'masked'" (qtd. in Lott 166). As with much of the cross-dressing examined in chapter 4, Schlissel suggests some titillation when dress and appearance highlight a covert sexuality, especially when the reality of the situation is understood so as to eliminate major fears. When the preposterous nature of the cross-dressing permitted "safe" impersonation, however, most audiences found the presentations raucously funny.

If satisfaction of spectatorial interest was reserved primarily to privileged white men, however, it is difficult to deny women's complicity in the spectatorial culture. Judith Mayne has suggested the impossibility of "separat[ing] the truly radical spectator from the merely complicitous one" (164). Women ensured the success of the fashion magazines and the spectatorial culture by admiring, coveting, and replicating the pleasurable look. Yet, recognizing the imbalance, many women and other less privileged persons and groups orchestrated scenes and expectations to influence reception of their appearance. In the case of women and dress, this was undoubtedly true. While women might be gazed upon at the opera, on the lawn, at the ball, they dressed the part in an effort to influence or control their impact on the looker; when assuming the platform, the most astute carefully staged the way they would be viewed in that situation as well.

The scopophilic culture actually served women speakers' purposes in two ways. First, as they changed places, women took with them knowledge gleaned from watching themselves being watched, making use of the abundant lessons they had absorbed. They often understood both intuitively and consciously the effect their appearance would have on an audience. They were thus able to use dress and appearance to their advantage. Second, reacting to their fear of lost scopophilic pleasure and accompanying fear of powerful women, reporters either reacted hysterically or attempted to return women to an appropriate location. Ironically, the frantic reaction and efforts to recapture the scopophilic loss supported the performative nature of women's appearances by providing the wide coverage of speakers that helped to normalize their roles as speakers and therefore their acceptance.

Newspapers' Complicity

As women changed attire and invaded places previously restricted to men, reporters sometimes acknowledged the scopophilic attraction. For example, when the *Cleveland Daily Plain Dealer* reported Emma Snodgrass's "parading in all the envelopes of masculine inhumanity," it also noted that "all deacons, and elders, and police magistrates, and the worthies of the land, have looked on and wondered, and wondered and gazed with some smack of the marvel experienced by the primitive elders who peeped after the chaste Susannah." Noting a preference for "a female petticoat to a female pantaloon" the *Plain Dealer* admitted that the daily occurrence of such "manifestations of freedom" caused some trepidation: "We tremble in our integuments lest some dark night some bold woman should stop us on the corner and demand either our pantaloons or our hands!" ("Women in Male Attire").

Expressed apprehensions of women's being masculinized or unsexed were clearly linked with their achieving power. Such outcries were accompanied by great fears of emasculation for men. One good example surfaces in an 1852 contribution to the *Knickerbocker*. Written by Thomas W. Lane, "Bloomerism: An Essay" claims that if woman adopts the Bloomer costume, "she will at last have unsexed herself" (242). Lane repeatedly uses terms associated with masculine virility, cautioning women that they will find the trousers either "too stiff" or "limbered" and that if they insist on assuming pants, the "bifurcate will cease to be the insignia of power, and men shall become impotent to hold their own!" (242). In an effort to return weakness to its rightful domain, Lane exclaims, "O Woman! Woman! Thy name is frailty: wilt thou make it folly?" and singles out for praise such women as Swisshelm and Partington, who refused to Bloomerize themselves. But, according to Lane, his own "sweet angel" assures him that she will not adopt the dress "and as she saith, she gazes modestly down upon the white and flowing robe which for centuries hath formed woman's best adornment" (242). Lane thus suggests that women's narcissism is laudable and is reassured that women will retain the dress of desire while modestly averting their own gaze in an appropriately downward direction.

Eventually, it seems, reporters' efforts focused primarily on attempts to return threatening women to a safety and pleasure similar to that of the parlor and pedestal. They re-created women speakers in detailed "pen pictures" and illustrations in newspapers and other popular periodicals, again focusing on the visual rather than the aural. Readers learned of the sensual nature of women speakers' appearance, from the color and texture of dresses to the gleam of gemstones and metals or the intricacy of laces and braids. Details about the color of hair, eyes, and complexion complemented descriptions of the shape of the mouth and the size of the body, hands, and feet. While recounting women's activities, reporters focused on them in a manner that allowed readers to mentally wander over their bodies to experience their material and sensual features, sometimes from head to toe, as in this description of Mrs. J. W. Stowe, head of the Social Science Sisterhood in San Francisco:

> Her hair is cut short and was bound up with a narrow blue ribbon. She wore a black velvet coat-tailed basque and a short black silk plaited skirt. The "line of beauty" was concealed by black cassimere trousers covering the instep. Her gaiters were of cloth, and on her breast was a red silk badge stamped S.S.S. and fastened with a diamond pin and two artificial roses. She carried a fan. ("A Lady Lecturer in Trousers")

Other times the movement was from bottom to top as in these examples from the World's Congress of Representative Women:

> Miss Cayvan wore a pretty costume of rose-pink silk, covered with black chiffon. The skirt was made with three lace insertions and the bodice had a yoke of lace, with a bertha of fine jet. The collar, belt, and cuffs were of lace. Her hair was dressed high, and she wore a large corsage bouquet of violet. She wore diamond ornaments. . . .
> Miss Marlowe wore a charming gown of pale blue soft silk, trimmed on the skirt with three clusters of bias bonds edged in black. The bodice was of black chiffon, covered with loose bands of blue silk edged with lace, and the large sleeves were of chiffon. Her hair was dressed low, with gold ornament, and she carried a large bouquet of white roses. ("What the Ladies Wore")

Descriptions moved up or down the body, returning to focus on accessories of particular interest, recalling earlier threats to women that their public participation removed traditional means by which they were protected. If women were concerned about such detailed reports, however, I have found no evidence of it. More likely they were either grateful for attention to themselves and their causes or thought it worthwhile to relinquish the pretended lack of spectatorship for one more openly acknowledged.

Although men may have recovered some pleasure as they could again look at women unacknowledged and undisturbed in the stationary and passive descriptions and illustrations, the highly visible efforts at reconstructing a reassuring and pleasurable spectacle also associated women with the public and political in the nation's consciousness, reconfiguring cultural conceptions. Imprisoned though they might be in print, in reality women were escaping the private pleasurable gaze and the numerous cultural constrictions that accompanied it.

Jo B. Paoletti and Claudia Brush Kidwell write, "Controversial fashion changes such as women adopting trousers can only take place after women's roles in society have altered. The mass acceptance of a style may accompany a change in public opinion, but does not precede it" (160). Paoletti and Kidwell see little success in the nineteenth-century dress reform movement, believing that reformers "erred in believing . . . changes in gender conventions would automatically follow" (160). Such interpretation dwells purely on the capacity of the movement to create changes in dress, and it effected minimal change initially. Seen in rhetorical terms, however, the Bloomer might be considered highly successful. The same may be said for the dress of women later in the century. If we see women speakers' change in dress as weak because reactive, perhaps that has more to do with the way we have gendered women than with the effectiveness of their rhetoric. In adapting dress to fit the times and mood of the country, women showed a remarkable rhetorical sophistication in recognizing what worked for them, discarding one dress as it became ineffective for one more useful. If the more effective style was a more conventionally feminine one, then the more feminine was the more powerful, and our perceptions of the "womanly" style as weak or as capitulation may reflect our own gender biases rather than the actual power of women's rhetoric.

The Importance of Dress in the Study of Rhetoric

We may read the works of our rhetorical foremothers and marvel at their eloquence, but to fully appreciate their rhetorical sophistication, we must understand the larger context with which they contended. When writing about public issues, and especially when speaking publicly, they necessarily forged new means of persuading audiences and negotiated perilous expectations not previously recognized in the western tradition of rhetoric. Differentiated according to gender, women found it imperative to create new methods for addressing audiences. In the nineteenth century, their deft attention to dress and appearance defined one means of adjusting rhetorical strategies to their own unique needs. No doubt we will learn of other impressive ways women adapted to rhetorical needs as scholars continue their efforts at constructing a more comprehensive understanding of our rhetorical tradition.

In examining women's use of dress for rhetorical purposes in the nineteenth century, a striking parallel stands out a century later. The second wave of feminism duplicates in many ways the dress associated with the movement for women's rights in the nineteenth century. Although dress was often influenced by ethnicity, region, and other factors, women in the 1950s, especially the "ideal woman" depicted in popular magazines and on television, dressed in a fashion that demonstrated an emphasis on body similar to that of the previous century, carefully matching dress with gender expectations and place. Crinolined skirts often accented small belted waists; strapless evening wear emphasized shoulders and cleavage. Women's and men's clothing differed greatly. Similarly, the 1950s offered the pretense that women occupied a protected place where lust and desire remained in the home, contained in the bedroom, if in that romanticized shelter at all. However, with the feminist movement of the late 1960s and 1970s, many women began to appropriate dress traditionally seen as belonging to men. Pantsuits became the vogue, and women began to wear trousers even for employment and public situations. Women's dress for success was the suit. Some sported tuxedolike dress or neckties that further stated their move into masculine spaces. In both centuries, women undressed the assumptions and categories that refused them public power and slowly but successfully redressed their relegation to the private.

NOTES
WORKS CITED
INDEX

Notes

Introduction: Fabricated Gender

1. Patricia Bizzell extended this discussion in her role as featured speaker at the 2000 Conference of the Rhetoric Society of America, a presentation reprinted in *Rhetoric Society Quarterly* 30 (Fall 2000): 5–17. See that reprint for a fuller discussion of this issue as well as for a more complete listing of those Bizzell sees as having contributed to these new approaches.

2. Dress is especially amenable to the notion of play and instability associated with space. Defined as clothing when a noun, as a verb *dress* means to arrange or align, in keeping with Foucault's grid. In order to keep one in place, it might be necessary to "dress down." Foucault actually defines his "technique for training" bodies as dressage (168).

3. Veblen elaborates:

> The dress of women goes even farther than that of men in the way of demonstrating the wearer's abstinence from productive employment. It needs no argument to enforce the generalization that the more elegant styles of feminine bonnets go even farther towards making work impossible than does the man's high hat. The woman's shoe adds the so-called French heel to the evidence of enforced leisure afforded by its polish; because this high heel obviously makes any, even the simplest and most necessary manual work extremely difficult. The like is true even in a higher degree of the skirt and the rest of the drapery which characterizes woman's dress. The substantial reason for our tenacious attachment to the skirt is just this: it is expensive and it hampers the wearer at every turn and incapacitates her for all useful exertion. The like is true of the feminine custom of wearing the hair excessively long. (171)

In addition to expense in construction and forced idleness, Veblen adds the requirement that dress be up to date as another factor in establishing differences between the classes.

4. On March 20, 1862, Chesnut reports overhearing two women discuss slaves' clothing:

One lady said (as I sit reading in the drawing-room window while Maum Mary puts my room to rights): "I clothe my Negroes well. I could not bear to see them in dirt and rags. It would be unpleasant for me." Another lady: "Yes, well, so do I, but not fine clothes, you know. I feel—now—it was one of our sins as a nation, the way we indulged them in sinful finery. We will be punished for it."

5. Loose-fitting Mother Hubbard dresses were suspect because of the easy access they permitted to women's bodies.

6. Ironically, Dr. Henry Whitney Bellows (1814–82), a Unitarian clergyman, was founder and president of the U.S. Sanitary Commission, an organization composed primarily of women during the Civil War. Women who participated in the Sanitary Commission played very public roles, often went onto the battlefields, and reported their activities in public addresses and written narratives. They could hardly be viewed as sheltered from the public gaze.

1. Friendly Dress: A Disciplined Use

1. The effectiveness of Quaker attire for women speakers was enhanced by its peculiarity, which immediately identified its wearer with feminine simplicity, modesty, and religious sincerity. Quaker apparel was not uniform in the sense of much religiously connoted dress (e.g., that of monks or nuns). It varied greatly in quality of fabric, for instance. However, the importance for my discussion is that Quaker dress was readily identifiable. For a look at the development of the distinctive form of Quaker dress, see Kendall.

I also recognize the significance of the "cultural seedbed" for activism that Quakerism provided for women. As Bacon suggests, "The institutionalization of the traveling ministry, the separate women's business meeting, and the concept of equal educational opportunities for women had laid the groundwork for the strides Quaker women were to make in reforms and professions in the decades ahead" (*Mothers* 100). I agree with the importance of this background. I believe, however, that such a preparation might encourage women's perceptive use of dress, as women's familiarity with dress could serve to reinforce propensities to activism.

2. Foucault cites Bentham as a major influence on his theories.

3. As noted in chapter 2, the immorality of women's showing of legs would become an issue later, at midcentury, when reformers adopted the Bloomer costume, a shortened dress with trousers beneath. Both nineteenth- and twentieth-century critics of dress often noted the impact of women's dress on mobility. Length of skirts, voluminous petticoats, and later hoops made movement difficult. Such restrictions, of course, limited women's "entry" both literally and figuratively.

4. See, e.g., Sterling 41, 114, 137, and 153 for Abby Kelley's attention to the Wright problem, and Barnes and Dumond 88 and 113 for examples pertaining to the Grimkés.

5. Amelia Opie (1769–1853), British novelist and widow of painter John Opie, joined the Society of Friends on 11 August 1825 at age fifty-five. The change in her lifestyle was often noted through metaphors of dress. Her friend, Lady Cork,

wrote her shortly after her reception into membership, affirming her continued affection and demonstrating the conventional association between dress and the Quaker religion:

> Will your primitive cap never dine with me, and enjoy a quiet society? but really, am I never to see you again? Your parliament friend does not wear a broad-brimmed hat; so pray, pray, *pray* do not put on the bonnet. So come to me and be my love, in a dove-coloured garb, and a simple head-dress. (Brightwell 217)

6. Similarly, popular schoolroom performance pieces depicted Quakers favorably. William Bentley Fowle, for example, presents a Quaker orator, Mr. Steady, as the moderator and moral leader in several of his performance pieces. Early women speakers capitalized on such perceptions, using simple Quaker dress to change the way their bodies were read.

7. There remains no known copy of this manuscript, but evidence from letters and diaries substantiate its onetime existence.

2. Blooming Celebrity: The Flowering of a National Ethos

1. In introducing "Our Fashion Plate" (fig. 2.3), Bloomer told her readers,

> We take pleasure in laying before our readers two styles of the new costume, for winter, as worn by ladies here and in other localities.
>
> A lengthy description of these fashions we deem unnecessary as they show for themselves what they are; but as we have been enquired of frequently what material was to be worn for winter, and in what style to be made, we will say that broadcloth, velvet, tweed and merinos are used according to the taste and means of the wearer. The dress is usually made with a yoke at the neck, and plaited waist, without bodice or whalebones and a full skirt set on with a belt or cord; or a plain waist, buttoned part way up in front and then left open displaying an under kerchief, or buff vest. There are other styles, but with these we are most familiar. The trowsers are worn both full and plain, according to choice. The full ones are more to our liking. We think them not as liable to get muddy as the plain straight ones, for the reason that they are gaged up several times and set closer about the ankles. They are made like children's drawers at the top—open at the sides, and button to a waist.

2. The sacque and bonnet are shown on the right of fig. 2.3. A sacque was similar to a paletot, or fitted jacket, but in keeping with the intentions of dress reform, the sacque was more loosely fitted. Like the paletot, the sacque was secured by buttons or other means so as to be less cumbersome than shawls or capes and to allow for the free use of hands.

3. Despite the fact that *Godey's* chose not to support the Bloomer, Sarah Hale had written an article for the *Lady's Book* as early as 1841 supporting its use for exercise: "The most suitable dress [for exercise] is unquestionably that which is

called Turkish, consisting of pantalettes or trowsers, and a short frock (the latter to be brought up sufficiently high on the bosom to prevent the exposure of the shoulders)" (Hale "How to Begin" 41). The same description applies to *Godey's* 1858 fashion plate.

4. In 1895 Willard published *How I Learned to Ride the Bicycle,* describing her efforts at bicycling and promoting exercise for women. An advocate of dress reform, Willard recognized that "a riding costume was a prerequisite" (75) for such activity and would necessitate changes in dress for women. According to Willard, "A reform often advances most rapidly by indirection. An ounce of practice is worth a ton of theory; and the graceful and becoming costume of woman on the bicycle will convince the world that has brushed aside the theories, no matter how well constructed, and the arguments, no matter how logical, of dress-reformers" (44).

3. Restraining Women's Rhetoric: Backlash Against the Reform Dress

1. During the time of the *Tribune's* most scurrilous attack on the Bloomer costume, Greeley was actually abroad, serving as commissioner at the World's Fair. However, he undoubtedly was aware of and acquiesced in the editorializing. Before the summer of 1851 had ended, the "Bloomer" had received a permanent name and a formidable opponent. Both made the dress an easier target for ridicule, and the precedent set by the nation's leading liberal newspaper made the costume and its wearers fair game for almost any others who wished to disparage it.

2. The epigraph at the beginning of this chapter serves as one example; another concocted letters from or to Theodosia E. Bang, M.A., M.C.P., +. ^. K., K.L.M. &c, &c. of Boston and included the following quip:

> We are emancipating ourselves, among other badges of the slavery of feudalism, from the inconvenient dress of the European female. With man's functions, we have asserted our right to his garb; and especially to that part of it which invests the lower extremities. With this great symbol, we have adopted others—the hat, the cigar, the paletot or round jacket. And it is generally calculated that the dress of the Emancipated American female is quite pretty,—as becoming in all points as it is manly and independent. I enclose a drawing made by my gifted fellow-citizen, INCREASEN TARBOX, of Boston, U.S., for *The Woman's Banner,* a periodical under my conduct, aided by several gifted women of acknowledged progressive opinions.

The criticism of credentialed women suggested in the letters following Bang's name, as well as the Boston *Woman's Banner,* a spoof on the American Woman Suffrage Association's *Woman's Journal,* located in Boston, clearly directs the humor at leaders in the movement for equal rights. The name Theodosia may have been taken from Theodosia Gilbert, a woman some claimed to be the first American woman to adopt the short dress and trousers. The fictional letter continued,

> I appeal to my sisters of the Old World, with confidence, for their sympathy and their countenance in the struggle in which we are engaged, and

which will soon be found among them also. For I feel that I have a mission across the broad Atlantic, and the steamers are now running at reduced fares. I hope to rear the standard of Female Emancipation on the roof of the Crystal Palace in London Hyde Park. Empty wit may sneer at its form, which is bifurcate. And why not? MOHOMET warred under the Petticoat of his wife KADIGA. The American female Emancipist marches on her holy war under the distinguishing garment of her husband. In the compartment devoted to the Unites States in your Exposition, my sisters of the old country may see this banner by the side of a uniform of female freedom . . . the garb of martyrdom for a month! the trappings of triumph for all ages of the future! ("Woman's Emancipation")

3. Louis A. Godey, founder of *Godey's Lady's Book*, bought Sarah Josepha Hale's *Ladies' Magazine* in 1837. At that time, Hale became literary editor of *Godey's*. As did other fashion magazines, *Godey's* assured its readers of women's input, and in 1841, it announced that it was a magazine "edited solely by ladies." Lydia Sigourney and Eliza Leslie both were named as editors at one time. Grace Greenwood was listed as an assistant editor, and she also edited *Godey's Lady's Dollar Newspaper*, a smaller offering that often served as a premium to encourage subscriptions to *Godey's Lady's Book*. There is little evidence to suggest much control by any of these women other than Hale. Still, because the journals repeatedly represented these women as active editors, most readers would have presumed their input on editorial matters.

4. *Godey's* had also contributed to negative attitudes toward the Bloomer in its fiction. In 1854 the periodical included a short story, "A Bloomer among Us," that presented a young Bloomer who was at one time mistaken for a boy and whom the people of Westbridge slighted by excluding from all social functions. The author commented on the "outrageous costume . . . in itself a sort of declaration of independence" (398) and justified the townspeople's treatment because "the ideas of the Bloomerites are many of them so flighty, and have so little reason or common sense to them" (402).

5. *Sartain's* was owned by John Sartain and William Sloanaker; *Sartain's* editor, Caroline Kirkland, had written numerous pieces for the magazine emphasizing the importance of dress reform prior to the excitement over the Bloomer. In August and September 1850, she wrote a two-part article entitled "The Significance of Dress" in which she attested to the importance of dress as a means of expression and as a manner of setting a tone of behavior. Kirkland was joined by John S. Hart as coeditor in 1851, but their tenure ended in June of that year, and the magazine had not commented on the reform dress during that period. During the second half of 1851, Dr. Reynell Coates served as editor, with Sartain himself becoming editor at the end of the year. So, during the greatest excitement over the Bloomer costume, there was no woman editor at *Sartain's*.

Peterson's, begun by Charles J. Peterson, an editor at *Graham's* and partial owner of the *Saturday Evening Post*, made a greater effort to accept the Bloomer than did the other fashion magazines. *Peterson's* was a $2 magazine, an effort by Peterson to draw subscribers from the more expensive $3 magazines such as *Godey's* and *Graham's*. Peterson made much of his magazine's value: original printings of writings, primarily by American authors, and colored fashion plates, at less cost than for other such magazines. Although the magazine boasted popular Ann S. Stephens as editor, there is reason to believe that Stephens had little actual editing control. She was the magazine's most frequent contributor, and her name appeared on each issue as editor, but Peterson often referred to her as coeditor; upon her death he recognized her as contributor but admitted she had been editor in name only. At any rate, Stephens sailed for Europe in April 1850, where she remained for two years, and she is unlikely to have influenced *Peterson's* stance on the costume (see *Peterson's* June 1850: 270).

6. Women did often move their legs in a circular motion in order to clear the long skirts from their path of movement (Kidwell 129). The *Peterson's* editor presented this as a matter of anatomy rather than necessity.

7. The importance of women's editorial posts is complicated, however, because female editors had varying degrees of authority. Still, since women editors were hired to present the image of a woman's magazine with a woman at the helm, many subscribers would have presumed women's participation in the magazines' editorial policies and, therefore, the attitudes assumed by the journals were often perceived to be that of influential women. The editorial policies are further complicated by the fact that the magazines competed for subscribers to a large extent by offering illustrations of the latest Paris fashions. Most, therefore, would have deemed the Bloomer a threat.

4. The Language of Passing and Desire: The Rhetoric of Cross-Dressing

1. Much recent excellent scholarship addresses cross-dressing. Marjorie Garber's work is perhaps most closely related to this discussion. As Garber notes, "The story of transvestism in western culture is in fact . . . bound up with the story of homosexuality and gay identity" (4). Garber's study and others examine transvestism primarily in its relationship to gay identity. The International Foundation for Gender Education estimates that of the 6 percent of the population that cross-dresses, 1 percent are transsexuals. The phenomenon provides a rich site for examining gender bending and a breadth of sexual identities, a fruitful and important discussion. However, such study is not within the scope of this project. In addition, our twenty-first-century perspectives, from a post-Freudian, postmodern consciousness, while capturing the complexities of sex and gender for our times, does not necessarily represent the equally complicated and different relationships and attitudes toward sex and gender in the nineteenth century. As Carroll Smith-Rosenberg has explained, "A different type of emotional landscape existed in the nineteenth century" (28). Smith-Rosenberg has illustrated the dangers of one culture imposing its views of gender and sexuality upon another from which it is separated by centuries. I agree with Smith-Rosenberg that we must recognize "a particular historical context" lest we distort the nature of others' intentions (8). In most

of the cross-dressing situations sited in this chapter, there simply is insufficient extant evidence to explain the full intent behind the cross-dressing to ensure that we do not confuse the reasons for individuals' behavior. My purpose here is to demonstrate the fascination with and visibility of cross-dressing in the nineteenth century in order to better understand the rhetorical impact of those who made use of cross-dressing for rhetorical purposes.

2. Stowe describes Susan as "a respectably dressed mulatto woman." Her turban is made "of the first quality, and her dress is neatly fitted, and of good material" (327). Emmeline, likewise, "is dressed with great neatness" (327). Susan recognizes the message her daughter's appearance affords: "Respectable families would be more apt to buy you, if they saw you looked plain and decent, as if you wasn't trying to look handsome" (329). Mr. Skeggs similarly acknowledges that Emmeline's curls, flowing loosely, "may make a hundred dollars difference in the sale of her" (330). Adolph dresses in "satin vest, gold guard chain, and white pants" (162). He serves as a double for St. Claire in his "negligent drollery" (162); his vest "stained with wine" represents the hedonistic intemperance in the St. Claire household. Contrasting the personalities of Marie and Augustine St. Claire, Stowe depicts Marie's anger at Rosa's daring to try on her dress—to assume a position above her station. The dress episode initiates the confrontation that leads to Rosa's being sent to a whipping-establishment and the hint that she will be stripped of modest and protective clothing. Most of the St. Claire slaves arrive at the slave warehouse with "sizable trunk[s] full of clothing" (325) that represent their status as privileged slaves—clothing the reader rightly discerns will surely and shortly be removed from them.

3. Capitola also changes clothing and identity with Claire, and Black Donald repeatedly assumes a new identity throughout the novel.

4. In a letter to William Still in reference to the underground railroad, Harper asks, "How fared the girl who came robed in male attire?" (qtd. in Sterling 162). The best-known example of passing was perhaps that of escaped slave Ellen Craft, who disguised herself as a white man and traveled successfully from Georgia to Boston with her husband, William, who pretended to be her slave.

5. For a chronological list of related fiction, see appendix 1, "A Chronological Listing of English and American Short Stories and Novels Featuring Cross-Dressing and Sex-Changing," in Richard Ekins and Dave King, eds., *Bending Genders: Social Aspects of Cross-Dressing and Sex-Changing* (New York: Routledge, 1996) 225–26.

6. Weber was following in the tradition of such artistic women as George Sand, who had gained much notoriety for her trousers and top hat. Sand herself emulated the actions of her mother and others, who dressed in trousers in order to gain entry to the cheap standing-room arenas of the theater's pit, an area reserved for men.

7. Walker married Albert Miller in 1856, retaining her birth name. The marriage was a short one. The couple separated in 1859 or 1860. The official divorce came some months later.

8. Later when she appeared in England, *All the Year Round* described her as follows:

It was curious to observe that, with all her strengths of mind, this lady had not been above making some concessions to that decorative instinct which is supposed to spring forever in the female breast. Those shortened skirts, of which so much has been said, were decorated with velvet trimmings; a sort of sash constructed of broad black ribbons was fastened in a large bow at the lady's back. She wore, moreover, a lace collar and white kid gloves and—greatest concession of all—had a wreath of flowers in her hair. ("M.D." 515)

9. According to the *Literary Digest,* Walker cut and sold her hair after the war "to help a woman who was financially embarrassed" ("Dr. Mary Walker's Eccentric Dress").

10. Rumors that Walker's medical appointment was a cover for spy activity surface repeatedly. Spiegel and Suskind support the rumor by reporting that "an October 1865 Judge Advocate General's report stated that Walker 'passed frequently beyond our lines far within those of the enemy, and at one time gained information that led General Sherman so to modify his strategic operations as to save himself from a serious reverse and obtain success where defeat before seemed to be inevitable'" (218).

11. The inscription on Walker's medal read as follows:

Whereas it appears from official reports that Dr. Mary E. Walker, a graduate of medicine, "has rendered valuable service to The Government, and her efforts have been earnest and untiring in a variety of ways," and that she was assigned to duty and served as an assistant surgeon in charge of female prisoners in Louisville, Ky., upon The recommendation of Major-Generals Sherman and Thomas and faithfully served as contract surgeon in The service of The United States, and has devoted herself with much patriotic zeal to The sick and wounded soldiers, both in The field and hospitals, to The detriment of her own health, and has endured hardships as a prisoner of war four months in a southern prison while acting as contract surgeon; and

Whereas by reason of her not being a commissioned officer in The military service a brevet or honorary rank can not, under existing laws, be conferred upon her; and

Whereas in The opinion of The President an honorable recognition of her services and sufferings should be made;

It is ordered. That a testimonial thereof shall be hereby made and given to The said Dr. Mary E. Walker, and that The usual medal of honor for meritorious services be given her.

Given under my hand in The city of Washington, D.C. this 11th day of November, A.D. 1865.

Andrew Johnson, President

By The President:
Edwin M. Stanton, Secretary of War.

The 1917 Board of Medal Award ruled the medal unwarranted, claiming the records provided no specific act or acts for which Walker had received the medal. In her refusal to relinquish either the original or replacement medals, she insisted, "One of them I will wear every day, and the other I will wear on occasions" (Snyder 53–54). The Medal of Honor was restored to her posthumously by President Jimmy Carter in 1977. She continues to be the only woman to have received this recognition. Today the medal is displayed in the Pentagon in the women's corridor (Williams).

12. If there was communication between the Empress Eugenie and Walker, there is no remaining evidence. Probably no such contact took place.

5. [Re]Fashioning a Proper Image by Dressing the Part

1. In their *History of Woman Suffrage,* Stanton and Anthony write, "It invoked so much ridicule, that they feared the odium attached to the dress might injure the suffrage movement, of which they were prominent representatives. Hence a stronger love for woman's political freedom, than for their own personal comfort, compelled them to lay it aside."

2. The flurry of reform activity at midcentury that accompanied the sensation over the reform dress was placed on hold as the country moved toward civil war. During the war, efforts to support the Union cause consumed much of reformers' time and energy, as well as press attention and interest in general. Following the war, in 1869, the Equal Rights Association, whose membership was composed primarily of early proponents of woman's rights, split over the issue of suffrage for black males. Stanton, Anthony, and members who would form the National Woman Suffrage Association (NWSA) opposed a fifteenth amendment to the Constitution that would extend suffrage to freed male slaves but not to women; Lucy Stone, Julia Ward Howe, and others who continued to demand that women be given the vote but who also supported the fifteenth amendment formed the American Woman Suffrage Association (AWSA). The leadership of the two groups differed greatly, but each sought to present an acceptable public image of its members. In addition, numerous other women's groups formed as the century advanced.

3. George Francis Train (1829–1904) subsidized Stanton and Anthony's *Revolution.* Their deference to Train is obvious in the large, favorable space they gave him in the early years of the *Revolution.* Train, a wealthy merchant, shipbuilder, author, and promoter, led a sensational life, traveling around the world and being arrested numerous times on charges ranging from disturbance of public meetings to obscenity. A relentless self-promoter, he espoused numerous radical causes, such as French communism and the Fenian movement to overthrow Britain's control of Ireland.

4. Because of her celebrity, Greenwood also had her person submitted to scrutiny. After a lecture in Columbus, Ohio, the *Madison State Journal* reported,

She looks neither girlish nor matronly, more like a maiden aunt than a wife and mother. She is about five feet three inches high, thin, with a narrow face, a good sized nose of her own, and a slight general resemblance to the "strong-minded." . . . She has dark hair and eyes, and in conversation her thin face seems to grow more intellectual, and to light up very sweetly. It is a pleasant disappointment to meet her off the platform. She is older than I had supposed, appearing perhaps thirty-five. ("Grace Greenwood" 3)

5. Lucy Thurman headed the WCTU's Department of Work among Colored People during much of the 1890s.

6. Truth's New York appearance was in 1853. Examples of Harper's similar identification can be found in the *Mobile Register* (30 July 1871), the *Newark Daily Advertiser* (27 October 1876: 2), the Philadelphia *Public Ledger* (3 November 1885: 4), and the *Baltimore Sunday Herald* (20 October 1895). Nancy Prince was so identified by the Philadelphia *Public Ledger* (20 October 1854: 1). Examples at the end of the century surface in reports concerning Ida B. Wells in the *Washington Post* (2 and 21 February 1893), the *New York Tribune* (30 June 1894: 7), and the New York *Sun* (30 July 1894); and Lucy Thurman in the *Cleveland Daily Plain Dealer* (18, 21, and 25 November 1894). Volume 1 of the *History of Woman Suffrage* was published in 1881.

Works Cited

"About Women." *Courier Journal* [Louisville] 19 Nov. 1872: 2.

"A. E. Grimké." *Liberator* 11 May 1838: 76.

"Angelina E. Grimké." *Liberator* 2 Mar. 1838: 35.

"Another Damsel in Pants." *Boston Herald* 3 Dec. 1852: 4.

"Another Girl in Pants." *Boston Herald* 22 Dec. 1852: 2.

"Approaching Change in Ladies' Dress." *Home Journal* 17 May 1851: 2.

"Arrest." *New York Times* 6 June 1866: 8.

"Arrested Again in Male Attire." *New York Times* 11 Nov. 1883: 3.

Bacon, Margaret Hope. *I Speak for My Slave Sister: The Life of Abby Kelley Foster.* New York: Crowell, 1974.

———. *Mothers of Feminism: The Story of Quaker Women in America.* San Francisco: Harper, 1986.

Barnes, Gilbert H., and Dwight L. Dumond, eds. *Letters of Theodore Dwight Weld, Angelina Grimké Weld, and Sarah Grimké, 1822–1844.* Vol. 1. New York: Appleton-Century, 1934. 2 vols.

Beecher, Catharine Esther. *An Essay on Slavery and Abolitionism with Reference to the Duty of American Females.* Philadelphia: Henry Perkins, 1837.

———. *Letters on the Difficulties of Religion.* Hartford: Belknap and Hammersly, 1836.

Beecher, Henry Ward. "Henry Ward Beecher on Bloomerism." *Water Cure Journal* Jan. 1855: 9.

Berger, John. *Ways of Seeing.* New York: Penguin, 1972.

Biesecker, Barbara. "Coming to Terms with Recent Attempts to Write Women into the History of Rhetoric." *Philosophy and Rhetoric* 25.2 (1992): 140–61.

Bizzell, Patricia. "Feminist Methods of Research in the History of Rhetoric: What Difference Do They Make?" *Rhetoric Society Quarterly* 4 (Fall 2000): 5–17.

———. "Opportunities for Feminist Research in the History of Rhetoric." *Rhetoric Review* 11.3 (1992): 50–58.

Blackwell, Alice Stone. *Lucy Stone: Pioneer Woman Suffragist.* Boston: Little, 1930.

Bloomer, Amelia. "Male Bloomers." *Lily* 1 Feb. 1854: 4.

———. "Mrs. Swisshelm." *Lily* Sept. 1851: 70.

———. "Mrs. Swisshelm Again." *Lily* Oct. 1851: 78.

Bloomer, D. C. *Life and Writing of Amelia Bloomer.* 1895. New York: Schocken, 1975.

"Bloomer among Us." *Godey's Lady's Book* May 1854: 396–402.

"Bloomer Ball." *Lily* Aug. 1851: 64.

"The Bloomer Ball." *London Times* 31 Oct. 1851.

"The Bloomer Costume." *Gleason's* June 1851: 104.

"The Bloomer Costume." *New York Herald* 2 July 1851: 2.

"Bloomer Costume Improved." *New York Daily Tribune* 20 Aug. 1851: 5.

"The Bloomer Dress." *Sartain's* Sept. 1851: 243.

"A Bloomer Festival." *New York Daily Tribune* 27 June 1851: 4.

"Bloomerism." *New York Daily Tribune* 1 July 1851: 6.

"Bloomerism." *New York Daily Tribune* 28 Aug. 1851: 5.

"Bloomerism." *Saturday Visiter* [Pittsburgh] 15 Nov. 1851: 170.

"Bloomerism in the Mills." *Lily* July 1851: 53.

"Bloomer Promenade." *Saturday Visiter* [Pittsburgh] 18 Oct. 1851: 154.

"Bloomers." *New York Daily Tribune* 19 Sept. 1851: 5.

"Bloomers." *New York Daily Tribune* 1 Oct. 1851: 7.

"The Bloomer Schottisch." *New York Daily Tribune* 18 July 1851: 4.

"Bloomers in California." *New York Daily Tribune* 14 Aug. 1851: 7.

"The Bloomers in Town." *New York Daily Tribune* 26 Aug. 1851: 4.

"Bloomer's Turkish Trowsers." *Madison Tribune,* qtd. in *New York Daily Tribune* 12 June 1851: 6.

Blum, Stella. Introduction. *Victorian Fashions and Costumes from* Harper's Bazar, *1867–1898.* New York: Dover, 1974.

"Book and Magazine Notices." *Sibyl* 15 July 1856: 11.

Bordo, Susan. *Unbearable Weight: Feminism, Western Culture, and the Body.* Berkeley: U of California P, 1993.

Boydston, Jeanne. "To Earn Her Daily Bread: Housework and Antebellum Working-Class Subsistence." *The History of Women in the United States,* vol. 4, *Domestic Ideology and Domestic Work.* Ed. Nancy Cott. New York: Saur, 1992. Pt. 1, 27–47.

Brightwell, Cecilia Lucy. *Memorials of the Life of Amelia Opie.* Norwich: Fletcher and Alexander, 1854.

Brody, Miriam. *Manly Writing: Gender, Rhetoric, and the Rise of Composition.* Carbondale: Southern Illinois UP, 1993.

Brown, William Wells. *Clotel; or, The President's Daughter: A Narrative of Slave Life in the United States.* London: Partridge and Oakey, 1853.

Buell, Caroline B. *The Helping Hand; or, The A-B-C of Organizing a WCTU.* Chicago: Woman's Temperance Publication Association, 1887.

"Bunnell and Price." *New York Daily Tribune* 1 July 1851: 1.

Burke, Kenneth. *A Rhetoric of Motives.* New York: G. Braziller, 1955.

Burleigh, Celia. "The Sisters Grimké." *Woman's Journal* 23 July 1870: 232.

"A Bustline Army of Crusaders." *Chicago Times* 26 Oct. 1877: 8.

Butler, Judith. *Gender Trouble: Feminism and the Subversion of Identity.* New York: Routledge, 1993.

Campbell, Karlyn Kohrs. *Man Cannot Speak for Her: A Critical Study of Early Feminist Rhetoric.* Vol. 1. Westport, CT: Greenwood, 1989. 2 vols.

"The Cause of the Crusade." *Inter-Ocean* [Chicago] 25 Oct. 1877: 8.

Ceplair, Larry. *The Public Years of Sarah and Angelina Grimké.* New York: Columbia UP, 1989.

"Change in Female Costume." *Oswego Journal,* qtd. in *New York Daily Tribune* 27 May 1851: 6.

Chesnut, Mary Boykin. *A Diary from Dixie.* Ed. Ben Ames Williams. Boston: Houghton, 1949.

"Chit-Chat of the August Fashions." *Godey's Lady's Book* Aug. 1851: 128.

"Chit-Chat with Readers." *Peterson's* Oct. 1851.

"City Items." *New York Daily Tribune* 26 June 1851: 5.

"A Colored Lady." *Lily* July 1851: 54.

Conboy, Katie, Nadia Medina, and Sarah Stanbury. *Writing on the Body: Female Embodiment and Feminist Theory.* New York: Columbia UP, 1997.

Conrad, Earl. *Harriet Tubman.* New York: Paul S. Eriksson, 1969.

Cooper, James Fenimore. *The Letters and Journals of James Fenimore Cooper.* Vol. 2. Ed. James Franklin Beard. Cambridge: Belknap, 1960. 6 vols.

"The Corseted Crusade." *Washington Post* 30 Oct. 1881: 2.

"Corset-Strings and Suffrage." *Revolution* Oct. 1870: 299.

"Costume." *Revolution* 18 Nov. 1869: 307.

"Daughter of a Slave Speaks." *Chicago Herald* 21 May 1893: 2.

Davis, Elizabeth L. *Lifting as They Climb: The National Association of Colored Women.* Washington, D.C.: National Association of Colored Women, 1933.

de Certeau, Michel. *The Politics of Everyday Life.* Trans. Steven Rendall. Berkeley: U of California P, 1984.

"Decorations." *Woman's Journal* 11 June 1870: 182.

"Donning Male Attire." *Boston Herald* 31 Dec. 1852: 4.

"Dress and Disease." *Philadelphia Ledger,* qtd. in *Saturday Visiter* 30 Aug. 1851: 1.

"Dress and the Victims." *Sibyl* 1 Dec. 1859: 662.

"Dress Reform and Moral Reform." *Woman's Journal* 31 May 1873: 170.

"Dress Reform in Chicago." *St. Louis Post-Dispatch* 21 Oct. 1884: 8.

"Dr. Mary Walker." *Spectator* 24 Nov. 1866: 1305–6.

"Dr. Mary Walker Arrested." *New York Times* 6 Dec. 1878: 2.

"Dr. Mary Walker's Eccentric Dress Drew Attention from Her Real Achievements." *Literary Digest* 15 Mar. 1919: 94.

"Dr. Walker Arrested Again." *New York Times* 2 Feb. 1913: 1.

Eckhardt, Celia Morris. *Fanny Wright, a Biography.* Cambridge: Harvard UP, 1981.

Eicher, Joanne B., and Mary Ellen Roach-Higgins. "Definition and Classification of Dress: Implications for Analysis of Gender Roles." *Dress and Gender.* Ed. Ruth Barnes and Joanne B. Eicher. Providence: Berg, 1992. 8–28.

"Emma Snodgrass." *Boston Herald* 11 Dec. 1852: 2.

"Emma Snodgrass." *Boston Herald* 15 Dec. 1852: 4.

"Emma Snodgrass." *Boston Herald* 18 Dec. 1852: 4.

"Emma Snodgrass." *Boston Herald* 22 Dec. 1852: 4.

"Emma Snodgrass." *Boston Herald* 29 Dec. 1852: 2.

"Fanny Wright's Sunday Theatre." *New York Daily Express* 1 Oct. 1838: 2.

"Fashionable Women." *Revolution* 2 Feb. 1881: 14.

"The Fashion Magazines." *Sibyl* 1 Dec. 1857: 276.

Fausto-Sterling, Anne. *Sexing the Body: Gender Politics and the Construction of Sexuality.* New York: Basic, 2000.

"Favorable Notices of the Press." *New York Daily Tribune* 12 June 1851: 6.

"Female Anti-Slavery Society." *Liberator* 3 Nov. 1837: 179.

"Female Attire." *Lily* Mar. 1851: 21.

"A Female in Breeches." *New York Daily Tribune* 22 Dec. 1852: 7.

"A Female in Pantaloons." *New York Daily Tribune* 28 Dec. 1852: 7.

"A Female Pedestrian." *New York Daily Tribune* 1 Nov. 1851: 6.

Fern, Fanny. "Lady Lecturers." 1870. *Ruth Hall and Other Writings.* Ed. Joyce W. Warren. New Brunswick: Rutgers UP, 1986. 369–70.

———. "A Law More Nice than Just." I and II. 1858. *Ruth Hall and Other Writings.* Ed. Joyce W. Warren. New Brunswick: Rutgers UP, 1986. 299–304.

"Fine Ladies Promenading." *New York Daily Times* 10 Nov. 1855: 3.

Fitch, Suzanne Pullon. "Sojourner Truth." *Women Public Speakers in the United States, 1800–1925.* Ed. Karlyn Kohrs Campbell. Westport, CT: Greenwood, 1993.

"For the Evening Post." *New York Evening Post* 12 Jan. 1829: 2.

Foss, Sonja K., Cindy L. Griffin, and Karen A. Foss. "Transforming Rhetoric Through Feminist Construction: A Response to the Gender Diversity Perspective." *Women's Studies in Communication* 20 (Fall 1997): 117–35.

Foucault, Michel. *Discipline and Punish.* New York: Random, 1979.

"From the Bay State Democrat." *Liberator* 18 Feb. 1842: 25.

"From the Evening Post." *New York Daily Express* 9 Oct. 1838: 2.

Gale, Xin Liu. "Historical Studies and Postmodernism: Rereading Aspasia of Miletus." *College English* 62 (Jan. 2000): 361–86.

Gambone, Joseph G. "The Forgotten Feminist of Kansas: The Papers of Clarina I. H. Nichols, 1854–1885." *Kansas Historical Quarterly,* pt. 5 (Spring 1974): 72–135. 6 parts.

Garber, Marjorie. *Vested Interests: Cross-Dressing and Cultural Anxiety.* New York: Routledge, 1991.

Gattey, Charles Neilson. *The Bloomer Girls.* New York: Coward-McCann, 1968.

Giddings, Paula. *When and Where I Enter: The Impact of Black Women on Race and Sex in America.* New York: Morrow, 1984.

Glenn, Cheryl. *Rhetoric Retold: Regendering the Tradition from Antiquity Through the Renaissance.* Carbondale: Southern Illinois UP, 1997.

Godey, Louis. "The New or Proposed New Costume." *Godey's Lady's Book* Sept. 1851: 189.

Gordon, Ann D., Mari Jo Buhle, and Nancy Schrom Dye. "The Problem of Women's History." *Liberating Women's History.* Ed. Berenice A. Carroll. Urbana: U of Illinois P, 1976. 75–92.

Gordon, Linda. "What's New in Women's History." *Feminist Studies/Critical Studies.* Ed. Teresa de Lauretis. London: Macmillan, 1988.

"Great Gathering of Women of New York." *New York Daily Tribune* 8 Feb. 1853: 5.

"The Great Trouser Movement." *Saturday Evening Post* 28 Dec. 1850: 2.

Greene, E. G., ed. *Pathfinder for the Organization and Work of the Woman's Christian Temperance Union.* Rev. ed. New York: National Temperance Society and Publication House, 1886.

Greenwood, Grace. "Grace Greenwood on the Washington Suffrage Convention." *Revolution* 4 Feb. 1869: 66–67.

Grimké, Sarah. "Dress of Women." *Liberator* 26 Jan. 1838: 16.

Grosz, Elizabeth. *Volatile Bodies: Toward a Corporeal Feminism.* Bloomington: Indiana UP, 1994.

Guy-Sheftall, Beverly. *Words of Fire: An Anthology of African-American Feminist Thought.* New York: New Press, 1995.

Hale, Sarah J. "How to Begin." *Lady's Book and Ladies' American Magazine* July 1841: 41–42.

Harper, Ida Husted. *The Life and Work of Susan B. Anthony.* Vol. 1. Indianapolis: Hollenbeck, 1898. 2 vols.

Hasbrouck, Lydia Sayer. "Lucy Stone's Position." *Sibyl* 15 Apr. 1859: 540.

Horowitz, Helen Lefkowitz. *Alma Mater: Design and Experience in the Women's Colleges from Their Nineteenth-Century Beginnings to the 1930s.* New York: Knopf, 1984.

"Hudibrastic Sketches." *Liberator* 8 Jan. 1847: 6.

"Ida Wells Heard Here." *Sun* [New York] 30 July 1894: 2.

"Influence of Woman." *Liberator* 15 Sept. 1837: 152.

"Insurrection of Petticoats." qtd. in Sterling 266.

"It Would Be More Healthy." *Lily* Sept. 1851: 66.

Jameson, Frederic. "Pleasure: A Political Issue." *Formations of Pleasure.* London: Routledge and Kegan Paul, 1983. 1–14.

Jarratt, Susan. "Comment: Rhetoric and Feminism Together Again." *College English* 62 (Jan. 2000): 390–93.

Kearney, Belle. *A Slaveholder's Daughter.* St. Louis: St. Louis Christian Advocate, 1900.

Kendall, Joan. "The Development of a Distinctive Form of Quaker Dress." *Costume* 1985: 58–74.

Kidwell, Claudia Brush. "Gender Symbols or Fashionable Details?" *Men and Women: Dressing the Part.* Ed. Claudia Brush Kidwell and Valerie Steel. Washington: Smithsonian Institution P, 1989. 124–43.

Kirkland, Caroline. "The Significance of Dress." *Sartain's* Aug. 1850: 99–102; Sept. 1850: 154–57.

"The Ladies' New Dresses." *New-Haven Palladium,* qtd. in *New York Daily Tribune* 27 May 1851: 6.

"A Lady Lecturer in Trousers." *Courier Journal* [Louisville] 22 Oct. 1882: 2.

"Lady Shangoes." *New York Daily Times* 10 Nov. 1855: 3.

Lane, Margaret. *Frances Wright and the "Great Experiment."* Manchester: Manchester UP, 1972.

Lane, Thomas W. "Bloomerism: An Essay." *Knickerbocker* Sept. 1852: 240–43.

Langer, Lawrence. *The Importance of Wearing Clothes.* New York: Hastings House, 1959.

Lathrap, Mary Torrans. *The Poems and Written Addresses of Mary T. Lathrap.* Ed. Julia R. Parish. Bay City: Woman's Christian Temperance Union of Michigan, 1893.

Lawrence, Leanna Michelle. *The Teaching of Rhetoric and Composition in the Nineteenth-Century Women's Colleges.* Diss. Duke U, 1990. Ann Arbor: UMI 1991DA9100120.

Lerner, Gerda. "The Lady and the Mill Girl: Changes in the Status of Women in the Age of Jackson." *The History of Women in the United States,* vol. 5, *The Intersection of Work and Family Life.* Ed. Nancy F. Cott. New York: Saur, 1992. Pt. 1, 32–43.

"Letter from A. F. Williams." *Liberator* 19 June 1840: 97.

"Local Events." *Baltimore and American Commercial Advertiser* 8 Nov. 1878: 4.

Logan, Olive. "A Word about Dress." *Revolution* 3 June 1869: 337.

Logan, Shirley Wilson, ed. *"We Are Coming": The Persuasive Discourse of Nineteenth-Century Black Women.* Carbondale: Southern Illinois UP, 1999.

——. *With Pen and Voice.* Carbondale: Southern Illinois UP, 1995.

"Long Skirts." *Phrenological Journal,* qtd. in *Lily* Dec. 1854: 176.

Lott, Eric. *Love and Theft: Blackface Minstrelsy and the American Working Class.* Oxford: Oxford UP, 1993.

Lumkin, Katharine De Pre. *The Emancipation of Angelina Grimké.* Chapel Hill: U of North Carolina P, 1974.

Lurie, Alison. *The Language of Clothes.* New York: Vintage, 1983.

"Male Bloomers." *Lily* 1 Feb. 1854: 4.

Massey, Mary Elizabeth. *Bonnet Brigades.* New York: Knopf, 1966.

Mattingly, Carol. *Well-Tempered Women: Nineteenth-Century Temperance Rhetoric.* Carbondale: Southern Illinois UP, 1999.

Mayne, Judith. "Paradoxes of Spectatorship." *Viewing Positions: Ways of Seeing Films.* Ed. Linda Williams. New Brunswick: Rutgers UP, 1995. 153–83.

McClellan, Elisabeth. *History of American Costume to 1870.* New York: Tudor, 1937.

McDowell, Colin. *Dressed to Kill: Sex, Power, and Clothes.* London: Hutchinson, 1992.

"M.D." *All the Year Round* 8 Dec. 1866: 514–16.

"The Metropolitan Gymnastic Costume." *Godey's Lady's Book* Jan. 1858: 68.

Michie, Helena. *The Flesh Made Word: Female Figures and Women's Bodies.* New York: Oxford UP, 1987.

Miller, Diane Helene. "The Future of Feminist Rhetorical Criticism." *Listening to Their Voices: Essays on the Rhetorical Activities of Historical Women.* Ed. Molly Meijer Wertheimer. Columbia: U of South Carolina P, 1997. 359–80.

Minutes of the First Convention of the National Woman's Christian Temperance Union, 1874. Chicago: Woman's Temperance Publication Association, 1889.

"Mirror of Fashion." *New York Daily Tribune* 28 Apr. 1851: 5.

"The Misses Grimké." *Liberator* 18 Aug. 1837: 135.

"Modern Crusaders." *Philadelphia Inquirer* 31 Oct. 1885: 2.

Morgan, Anna. "The Art of Elocution." *Congress of Women Held in the Woman's Building, World's Columbian Exposition, Chicago, U.S.A., 1893*. Philadelphia: S. I. Bell, 1894. 597–98.

"Movements of Emma Snodgrass." *New York Daily Tribune* 23 Dec. 1852: 7.

"Mrs. Bloomer's Address." *Cleveland Daily Plain Dealer* 4 Oct. 1853: 3.

"Mrs. Cady Stanton." *Louisville Commercial* 17 Nov. 1872: 2.

"Mrs. Kemble and Her New Costume." *Lily* 1 Dec. 1849: 94.

"Mrs. Sojourner Truth." *New York Daily Tribune* 5 Sept. 1853: 5.

Nevin, William. "The Bloomer Dress." *Ladies' Wreath* (1852): 247–55.

"A New Bloomer." *Cleveland Daily Plain Dealer* 14 Aug. 1852: 2.

"The New Costume." *Lily* Sept. 1851: 66–67.

"The New Costume for Ladies." *Telegraph* [Washington, D.C.], qtd. in *New York Daily Tribune* 27 May 1851: 6.

"The New Costume for Ladies." *New York Daily Tribune* 12 June 1851: 6.

"The New Costume for Ladies." *New York Daily Tribune* 24 June 1851: 3.

"The New Costume—How It Takes to the Rural Districts." *New York Daily Tribune* 21 May 1851: 6.

"The New Dress Question." *New York Daily Tribune* 3 June 1851: 7.

"The New Fashion for Ladies' Dress." *New York Daily Tribune* 27 May 1851: 6.

"The New Female Costume." *New York Daily Tribune* 27 May 1851.

"The New Female Costume." *New York Daily Tribune* 3 June 1851.

"The New Female Dress." *New York Herald* 15 June 1851: 1.

"New Officers Chosen at the Colored Women's Convention." *Chicago Tribune* 17 Aug. 1899: 8.

"Notable Women." *St. Louis Post-Dispatch* 24 Oct. 1884: 1–2.

O'Connor, Lillian. *Pioneer Women Orators: Rhetoric in the Ante-Bellum Reform Movement*. New York: Columbia UP, 1954.

"Our Dress." *Lily* May 1851: 38.

"Our Fashion Plate." *Lily* Jan. 1852: 1.

Painter, Nell Irvin. *Sojourner Truth: A Life, a Symbol*. New York: Norton, 1996.

Paoletti, Jo B., and Claudia Brush Kidwell. "Conclusion." *Men and Women: Dressing the Part*. Ed. Claudia Brush Kidwell and Valerie Steele. Washington: Smithsonian Institution P, 1989.

Pease, Jane H., and William H. Pease. *Bound Up with Them in Chains: A Biographical History of the Antislavery Movement*. Westport, CT: Greenwood, 1972.

Peterson, Carla L. *"Doers of the Word": African-American Women Speakers in the North, 1830–1880*. New York: Oxford UP, 1995.

"Petticoats and Pantiloons." *Les Libre* [New Orleans], qtd. in *Revolution* 25 Jan. 1868: 395.

"Petticoats at the Bar." *Revolution* 8 July 1869: 7.

Phelps, Elizabeth Stuart. *What to Wear?* Boston: James R. Osgood, 1873.

"Politicians in Petticoats." *Washington Post* 18 Feb. 1893: 8.

"A Question of Dress in San Francisco." *San Francisco Bulletin* 18 May 1866: 2.

Raiskin, Judith L., ed. *Wide Sargasso Sea.* New York: Norton, 1999.

"Religious." *Baltimore and American Commercial Advertiser* 7 Nov. 1878: 4.

"The Revolution in Dress." *New York Daily Tribune* 12 June 1851: 4.

Roberts, Helene E. "The Exquisite Slave: The Role of Clothes in the Making of the Victorian Woman." *Signs* 2 (Spring 1977): 554–69.

Robinson, Amy. "It Takes One to Know One: Passing and Communities of Common Interest." *Critical Inquiry* 20 (Summer 1994): 715–36.

Rossing, John Paul. *A Cultural History of Nineteenth-Century American Sabbath Reform Movements.* Diss. Emory U, 1994. Ann Arbor: UMI, 19945510A3215.

Sánchez-Eppler, Karen. *Touching Liberty: Abolition, Feminism, and the Politics of the Body.* Berkeley: U of California P, 1993.

Scott, Joan Wallach. *Gender and the Politics of History.* New York: Columbia UP, 1988.

Sedgwick, Catharine Maria. *Hope Leslie.* 1827. Ed. Mary Kelley. New Brunswick: Rutgers UP, 1987.

"She Pleads for Her Race." *New York Tribune* 30 June 1894: 7.

"Short Dresses." *Lily* June 1851: 46.

"Short Dresses in Milwaukee." *Milwaukee Advertiser,* qtd. in *New York Daily Tribune* 27 May 1851: 6.

"The Short-Skirt Affair in the Bowery." *New York Daily Tribune* 27 June 1851: 4.

Smith, Sidonie. *Subjectivity, Identity, and the Body: Women's Autobiographical Practices in the Twentieth Century.* Bloomington: Indiana UP, 1993.

Smith-Rosenberg, Carroll. "The Female World of Love and Ritual: Relations Between Women in Nineteenth-Century America." *Signs* 1 (1975): 1–29.

Snyder, Charles McCool. *Dr. Mary Walker: The Little Lady in Pants.* New York: Arno, 1974.

"Sojourner Truth." *Revolution* 28 Jan. 1869: 44.

"Sojourner Truth on the Fashions." *Woman's Journal* 12 Nov. 1870: 356.

"Some Elegant Costumes Worn." *Chicago Tribune* 16 May 1893: 2.

Southworth, E. D. E. N. *The Hidden Hand.* 1859. Ed. Joanne Dobson. New Brunswick: Rutgers UP, 1988.

Spiegel, Allen D., and Peter B. Suskind. "Mary Edwards Walker, M.D.: A Feminist Physician a Century Ahead of Her Time." *Journal of Community Health* June 1996: 211–35.

"The Spirit of Slavery Triumphant in Connecticut." *Liberator* 29 May 1840: 86.

Stanton, Elizabeth Cady. "More about Dress." *Revolution* 22 July 1869: 35.

Stanton, Elizabeth Cady, Susan B. Anthony, and Matilda Joslyn Gage. *The History of Woman Suffrage.* Vol. 1. 1881. Rochester: Charles Mann, 1889. 6 vols.

Steele, Valerie. *Fetish: Fashion, Sex, and Power.* New York: Oxford UP, 1996.

Sterling, Dorothy. *Ahead of Her Time: Abby Kelley and the Politics of Antislavery.* New York: Norton, 1991.

Stowe, Harriet Beecher. "Sojourner Truth, the Libyan Sibyl." *Atlantic Monthly* Apr. 1863: 473–81.

———. *Uncle Tom's Cabin.* 1851. New York: Bantam, 1981.

"Suffrage Convention." *Revolution* 4 Feb. 1868: 66.

"The Suffragists." *Courier Journal* [Louisville] 27 Oct. 1881: 2.

Swisshelm, Jane Grey. "The Bloomer Costume." *Saturday Visiter* [Pittsburgh] 26 July 1851: 106.

———. "The Bloomer Dress." *Saturday Visiter* [Pittsburgh] 20 Sept. 1851: 138.

———. "The Follies of Woman's Dress." *Independent* 24 July 1873: 924.

———. "The Journal and Bloomer Dress." *Saturday Visiter* [Pittsburgh] 4 Oct. 1851: 146.

———. "The Post and the Bloomers." *Saturday Visiter* [Pittsburgh] 8 Jan. 1853: 102.

———. "Short Dresses." *Saturday Visiter* [Pittsburgh] 17 May 1851: 66.

———. "Women in Male Attire." *Saturday Visiter* [Pittsburgh] 15 June 1850: 2.

———. "Women in Male Attire." *Saturday Visiter* [Pittsburgh] 10 May 1851: 26.

Tallant, Robert. *Romantic New Orleanians.* New York: Dutton, 1950.

"Tar for Dr. Mary Walker." *New York Times* 26 Oct. 1913: 1.

Tate, Claudia. *Domestic Allegories of Political Desire: The Black Heroine's Text at the Turn of the Century.* New York: Oxford UP, 1992.

"Temperance Women." *Chicago Evening Journal* 24 Oct. 1877: 4.

"They Flirt Their Flounces and Caps on the Platform." *Woman's Journal* 5 May 1871.

Thomas, Benjamin Platt. *Theodore Weld: Crusader for Freedom.* New Brunswick, NJ: Rutgers, 1950.

Thompson, Rev. Joseph. "Beware of Large Hands." *Revolution* 7 Oct. 1869: 217.

Thorp, Margaret Farrand. *Female Persuasion: Six Strong-minded Women.* New Haven: Yale UP, 1949.

"To Female Anti-Slavery Societies Throughout New England." *Liberator* 9 June 1837: 95.

"To Mr. Justice Wyman, Chief Justice of Police." *New York Evening Post* 5 Jan. 1829: 2.

"To the Editor of the Evening Post." *New York Evening Post* 12 Jan. 1829: 2.

Tower, Samuel A. "A Commemorative for Civil War Surgeon." *New York Times* 13 June 1982, sec. 2: 50.

Townsend, Fannie Lee. "Women in Male Attire." *Holden's Dollar Magazine* Mar. 1850: 178–79.

Train, George Francis. "Letters from Geo. Francis Train." *Revolution* 8 Oct. 1868: 215.

"Trousers for Women." *New York Times* 8 Mar. 1884: 5.

"The Turkish Costume." *Rochester Daily Times* and *Syracuse Journal,* qtd. in *New York Daily Tribune* 27 May 1851: 6.

"Varieties of Dress." *New York Daily Tribune* 11 June 1851: 4.

Veblen, Thorstein. *The Theory of the Leisure Class: An Economic Study of Institutions.* 1899. New York: Modern Library, 1934.

Watterson, Henry. *"Marse Henry": An Autobiography.* New York: George H. Doran, 1919.

"WCTU." *Newark Daily Advertiser* 27 Oct. 1876: 2.

"We Are Glad." *New York Commercial Advertiser,* qtd. in *Liberator* 11 May 1838: 82.

Wells, Ida B. *Crusade for Justice: The Autobiography of Ida B. Wells.* Ed. Alfreda M. Duster. Chicago: U of Chicago P, 1970.

"We May Owe an Apology." *Lily* July 1851: 55.

"We Predict." *Prattsville Advocate* [New York], qtd. in *New York Daily Tribune* 12 June 1851: 6.

Wertheimer, Molly Meijer, ed. *Listening to Their Voices: Essays on the Rhetorical Activities of Historical Women.* Columbia: U of South Carolina P, 1997.

"We Understand." *New York Daily Tribune* 3 Jan. 1853: 7.

White, Shane, and Graham White. *Stylin': African American Expressive Culture from Its Beginnings to the Zoot Suit.* Ithaca: Cornell UP, 1998.

"White Ribbons Wave." *Chicago Times* 17 Nov. 1894: 6.

Willard, Frances Elizabeth. "Dress and Vice." Chicago: Woman's Temperance Publication Association, n.d.

———. *How I Learned to Ride the Bicycle: Reflections of an Influential Nineteenth-Century Woman.* 1895. Ed. Carol O'Hare. Sunnyvale, CA: Fair Oaks, 1991.

"The Willard Dress." Frances E. Willard Memorial Library and WCTU Headquarters, Evanston, IL. N.p., n.d.

Williams, Rudi. "Only Woman Medal of Honor Holder Ahead of Her Time." *DefenseLink: U.S. Department of Defense.* http://www.defenselink.mil/news/Apr1999/n04301999_9904304.html.

"Wine Is Their Foe." *Chicago Daily Tribune* 17 Nov. 1894: 1.

Wittenmyer, Annie. *History of the Woman's Crusade.* 1878. Boston: J. H. Earle, 1882.

"The Woman in Trousers." *New York Times* 22 Feb. 1882: 3.

"A Woman Recently." *Sibyl* June 1858: 340.

"Woman's Congress." *Chicago Herald* 16 May 1893: 1.

"Woman's Emancipation." *Punch* 21 (1851): 3.

"The Woman's Rights Convention." *New York Herald* 11 Sept. 1852: 3.

"Woman Suffrage." *New York Times* 12 May 1870: 8.

"Woman Suffrage." *Courier Journal* [Louisville] 9 Oct. 1881: 14.

"The Woman Suffrage Movement." *Courier Journal* [Louisville] 24 Oct. 1881: 14.

"Woman Suffragists." *Indianapolis Journal* 26 May 1880: 3.

"The Woman Who Wore Men's Clothes." *New York Times* 21 Feb. 1882: 3.

"Women in Male Attire." *Cleveland Daily Plain Dealer* 25 Oct. 1853: 2.

"The Women of Philadelphia." *Public Ledger and Daily Transcript* [Philadelphia], qtd. in Stanton et al. 804.

"Women's Dress." *New York Daily Tribune* 18 Aug. 1851: 6.

"Women's Rights and Duties—False Pride and Household Service." *New York Daily Tribune* 28 Oct. 1851: 4.

"Women's Scramble for the Breeches." *Rutland Herald,* qtd. in Stanton et al. 173.

"Women: Their Theme." *Chicago Daily Tribune* 19 May 1893: 4.

Woodward, Helen Beal. *The Bold Women.* New York: Farrar, 1953.

Wyman, Mary Alice. *Selections from the Autobiography of Elizabeth Oakes Smith.* Lewiston, ME: Lewiston Journal, 1924.

———. *Two American Pioneers: Seba Smith and Elizabeth Oakes Smith.* New York: Columbia UP, 1927.

Yee, Shirley J. *Black Women Abolitionists: A Study in Activism.* Knoxville: U of Tennessee P, 1992.

"A Young Lady Dressed in Male Apparel." *Public Ledger* [Philadelphia] 7 May 1836: 2.

"The Young Lady in Pants." *Cleveland Daily Plain Dealer* 3 Jan. 1853: 3.

"A Young Lady of Romantic Disposition." *Boston Herald* 8 Dec. 1852: 4.

Index

abolitionists, 20–25, 27, 30, 35, 71, 126
African American women, 5–6, 73, 153n.
4; Bloomer costume and, 110–11; and
class issues, 124–25, 128; and cross-
dressing, 86, 88–89, 153n. 4; and dress,
11–12, 109, 147–48n. 4; and femininity, 124, 126, 133; and organizations,
123–31; as true women, 131–34. *See
also* slavery
Albany Knickerbocker, 66, 141
All the Year Round, 95, 153–54n. 8
Amazons, 138
American (Rochester), 72–73
American Anti-Slavery Society, 27
American Free Dress League, 123
American Woman Suffrage Association
(AWSA), 15, 121–23, 129, 155n. 2
Anthony, Susan B., xv, 40, 155n. 2; Bloomer
costume and, 49–50, 107–9; NWSA
dress and, 118–19
appearance, 10, 18–20
"Art in Dress" (Miller), 112–13
artistic women, 89–91, 153n. 6
Aspasia, 3–4
Atlantic, 59–60
Aub, A. E. "Ted," xv
Austen, Harriet, 80
"Awakening of the Afro-American Woman,
The" (Matthews), 131
AWSA. *See* American Woman Suffrage As-
sociation (AWSA)

Bacon, Margaret Hope, 31, 148n. 1

*Baltimore and American Commercial Adver-
tiser,* 113–14
Baltimore Herald, 133
Bancroft, George, 14
Bang, Theodosia E., 150–51n. 2
Barnes, Gilbert H., 31
Barnum, P. T., 139–40
Bay State Democrat, 30, 36
Beach, Moses, 50
Beecher, Catharine, 21–22, 34
Beecher, Henry Ward, 38, 60
Bellows, Henry Whitney, 15, 148n. 6
biblical references, 32, 48
bicycle, 150n. 4
Biesecker, Barbara, 2
Bizzell, Patricia, 1, 4, 147n. 1
Blackwell, Alice Stone, 41, 49
Blackwell, Henry, 71
Bloomer, Amelia, 40–45, 73, 97, 149n. 1;
challenges to negative stereotypes, 47–
49; physical appearance and, 46, 49;
Swisshelm and, 51–58
Bloomer, D. C., 45–46
Bloomer costume, 14, 37–38, 143, 148n. 3,
149n. 1; abandonment of, 107–9; African American women and, 110–11;
backlash and, 66, 67–69; and Bloomer
activities, 63–66; description of, 41–43;
femininity and, 46, 49–50; and harassment of women, 69–73, 107–8; as immoral, 68–69, 72; names of, 69–70; national conversation on, 39–40; ridicule of, 72–73; support for, 62–66; tradi-

Carol Mattingly is an associate professor of English and the director of the University Writing Center at the University of Louisville. She is the author of *Well-Tempered Women: Nineteenth-Century Temperance Rhetoric* and the editor of *Water Drops from Women Writers: A Temperance Reader.*

Studies in Rhetorics and Feminisms

S tudies in Rhetorics and Feminisms seeks to address the interdisciplinarity that rhetorics and feminisms represent. Rhetorical and feminist scholars want to connect rhetorical inquiry with contemporary academic and social concerns, exploring rhetoric's relevance to current issues of opportunity and diversity. This interdisciplinarity has already begun to transform the rhetorical tradition as we have known it (upper-class, agonistic, public, and male) into regendered, inclusionary rhetorics (democratic, dialogic, collaborative, cultural, and private). Our intellectual advancements depend on such ongoing transformation.

Rhetoric, whether ancient, contemporary, or futuristic, always inscribes the relation of language and power at a particular moment, indicating who may speak, who may listen, and what can be said. The only way we can displace the traditional rhetoric of masculine-only, public performance is to replace it with rhetorics that are recognized as being better suited to our present needs. We must understand more fully the rhetorics of the non-Western tradition, of women, of a variety of cultural and ethnic groups. Therefore, Studies in Rhetorics and Feminisms espouses a theoretical position of openness and expansion, a place for rhetorics to grow and thrive in a symbiotic relationship with all that feminisms have to offer, particularly when these two fields intersect with philosophical, sociological, religious, psychological, pedagogical, and literary issues.

The series seeks scholarly works that both examine and extend rhetoric, works that span the sexes, disciplines, cultures, ethnicities, and sociocultural practices as they intersect with the rhetorical tradition. After all, the recent resurgence of rhetorical studies has not so much been a discovery of new rhetorics; it has been more a recognition of existing rhetorical activities and practices, of our newfound ability and willingness to listen to previously untold stories.

The series editors seek both high-quality traditional and cutting-edge scholarly work that extends the significant relationship between rhetoric and feminism within various genres, cultural contexts, historical periods, methodologies, theoretical positions, and methods of delivery (e.g., film and hypertext to elocution and preaching).

Queries and submissions:
Professor Cheryl Glenn, Editor
    E-mail: cjg6@psu.edu
Professor Shirley Wilson Logan, Editor
    E-mail: Shirley_W_Logan@umail.umd.edu
Studies in Rhetorics and Feminisms
    Department of English
    142 South Burrowes Bldg
    Penn State University
    University Park, PA 16802-6200